Table of Contents

Stoicism Made Simple

Find Your Inner Peace—A Step-by-Step Guide to Reduce Stress, Become More Resilient and Live a Happier Life

Terry Cole

Introduction

Don't confuse complex with difficult. Most situations are simple—many just emotionally difficult to act upon. —Timothy Ferris

Stoicism is, in fact, quite simple. This doesn't mean it is a comfortable path.

These two words seem to have become completely replaceable one for the other, but not in the case of stoicism. Throughout this book, or when next confronting a difficult situation, remember this statement: *Simple, not easy.*

The philosophy of stoicism is certainly not an endless state of musings and contemplations on life. Neither is a sorrowful enduring of what life may throw at you. With a proper stoical mindset and guidance, stoicism provokes a person to take action. This book aims to do that: to share and help apply the wisdom others have learned through their achievements, failures, habits, and strategies.

At first, stoicism might sound like a big word, a difficult concept. Philosophy is usually considered a contemplative action destined just for a group of thoughtful, reflective people. This is a common misconception about philosophy in general, and about stoicism in particular. Nonetheless, every aspect of our life encompasses a philosophical attitude. We all have a way to understand the world around us. Even if we are not aware of it, we have a set of ideas that shapes our beliefs and behaviors, our opinions about things and people, and the possibilities of having projects for the future. That is nothing less than our philosophy of life.

Stoicism is about learning that life is brief, ephemeral, and marvelous. There are very few certainties in life, and one of them is that we only have one. So, stoicism is about deciding how you want to live your only precious life. While this thought might be discouraging, stoicism teaches us to use it as a positive incentive to thrive and feel happier.

There is good and bad, lights and shadows, joy and pain. Stoicism is not a promise of endless cheerfulness because its foundations are grounded in truth. The first lesson to learn is that a fulfilling existence has all those components. It isn't about ignoring or avoiding the pitfalls you will find. That is too stressful. Stoicism is about learning that everything is movement, change, ups and downs, and—most important—that you are powerful enough to cope with it.

This book does not intend to be a traditional "self-help" book. Stoicism is *simple, not easy.* Therefore, you can't expect to find a simple recipe to implement in your life and see your problems fade away. These pages are an invitation to a wonderful journey that will help you develop a different and empowered vision of life.

The core foundation of stoicism is understanding, and from there, being able to distinguish and separate what you *can't* control from what you *can* control. Training yourself to move away from *reacting*, standing at a place of overwhelming emotion, to *facing* challenges from a place of self-confidence and reasoning. Once you master how to focus completely on what you *can* control, you will find that improving those unsatisfying aspects of your life is solely *your* responsibility. External circumstances can't change this!

Take this as an empowering statement: You are authorizing yourself to let go of those things you can't change, and realizing that nothing and no one can distract you from becoming the best version of yourself.

That's it. That is the hardest part, the challenging path of stoicism: It demonstrates that only you are kept accountable for everything in your life. You might be thinking by now about all the obstacles you permanently find in your way. Stoicism encourages you to withstand and don't let go of them by showing that those *roadblocks* are nothing but mere illusions. It doesn't mean they aren't real, but they aren't there to stop you. Instead, you are being challenged to break your glass ceiling.

Now there is in front of you the opportunity to move on, exercise the mental muscle, and learn how to extract the best and essential lessons from any situation. This book is here to help you take your first steps into the stoicism path. It is like learning to walk or to ride a bike: Once you learn, it becomes a part of you. It lays out the foundational elements of stoicism, and the importance of a mindset aligned with them. Then, you have to keep practicing and lifting after every fall.

Although the focus is set on the practical application of concepts or historical figures, we shall introduce how stoicism was initiated, the social context, and how it has been able to adapt through the passing of time. In fact, stoicism didn't change: It is just suitable for anyone, at any moment, at any place.

The essential point of this philosophical approach is to take action. For this purpose, this book consists of two main parts:

The first part is important as it explains what stoicism is, its core principles, and how people have made it their philosophy of life under different circumstances. It doesn't intend to be a philosophy class, yet it is useful to have some acquaintance with these ideas that might be new. If you watch a soccer match, you will probably have fun, but you will enjoy it more if you know the rules and how the game goes. These chapters will help you become conscious of possible struggles, limitations created by your mind, and fears by understanding the four key virtues of stoicism and mastering the art of knowing how to differentiate what you can control from what you can't.

Then, we will introduce you to the relevant figures of stoicism. The first reason to include a brief picture of the four former Stoics' lives is to highlight that people from all walks of life can apply this philosophy. And secondly, the secret ingredients for a stoical life lie not in the challenges they faced, but in how they *prepared*—not *reacted*—for when those challenges *did appear*. Life is a constant journey of growth and learning. Challenges and failures make this journey all the more enriching.

After this theoretical introduction that will present and clear up the concepts for you, we shall dedicate the rest of the book to developing practical applications. The second part describes and explains practical exercises and techniques to transform ideas into action. You will not only learn how a Stoic thinks, but how to behave like one.

In this part, you will find plenty of practical reflections, applications, and guidelines on three things:

- how to manage stress, see it as a friend, and as a result of this perspective, reduce its impact on your daily life.

- how to become more resilient: How to withstand shocking or painful situations, and healthily recover from them.

- how to live a happier life: Enjoy your life in which your values and dreams are aligned with who you are, and what you do daily, to reach the set of personal objectives you settled for yourself.

In the end, what's the purpose of all these efforts to simply learn? Developing a Stoic mindset is the end result. Being in the game, in life.

And nothing can stop you. Isn't that powerful?

What Is the Starting Point To Becoming a Stoic?

When you ask yourself what major challenges are you facing now, do you have a clear answer? Do you feel confident enough to confront them? If you are struggling as a parent, partner, business owner, worker, or entrepreneur, do you feel equipped enough to deal with the gazillion challenges these all can throw at you? A primary answer would be, *Even if I lack self-confidence, I still must solve these issues!* Most of us don't even stop to think about everything that is going on; We are just carried along by the stream of a wild routine. Do you ever feel like you are dragged from one day into another without being able to control anything?

The problem isn't that you don't know how to face the challenge; the problem is that you can't define it properly, or may not even be conscious of it. It is a matter of perspective: Are you living from a place of reaction, of constantly trying to not be tossed around by waves? Or do you choose a place of being prepared and ready to take on the wave?

Life doesn't take breaks, so you have to move on whether you are ready or not. This usually leads you to react or make decisions without too much thinking, or perhaps, avoiding those decisions and waiting for time to make trouble fade away. In the meantime, you might retreat into confounding behaviors to distract yourself. Are you avoiding challenges by temporarily pacifying yourself with things or situations that, deep down, you know are unsatisfying? If you're thinking *Yes, I'm definitely drinking too much, and putting off that decision*, consider this: The problem isn't the drinking, that is just a symptom. You are not seeing the forest for the trees.

The real underlying problem is being aware of what is the *cost* of that inactivity, of not making that decision, in the mid to long term. The decision to take action is the real struggle. And, *Yes, you can.* It won't be easy, but it is simple.

Consider these Stoic-oriented questions as an introduction to the power of stoicism.

Chapter 1:

What Is Stoicism and How Did It Come To Be?

Before we start, we shall anticipate that what you are about to read isn't a historical essay. A brief narration about the society where stoicism began will serve as an introduction to how its principles were incorporated into daily life, back when the first Stoics walked the streets of Athens, and later, Ancient Rome. The social context influences every system of ideas, and there is no way to understand them if we don't know how or why people need them.

Stoicism has its origins in Ancient Greece, a civilization that arose over two and half thousand years ago in the Balkan peninsula and the west coast of the current Republic of Turkey, surrounding the Aegean sea. They were called Greeks by the Romans, who, by the way, assimilated many cultural nuances when the Empire occupied the region. The Greeks were, in fact, Hellens. Our western civilization owes to the Hellens the great legacy that has shaped our way of life: the theater, the Olympics, democracy, and philosophy.

The Hellenistic civilization was able to develop arts and science, and have a political system that incentivized citizens' participation because of their social organization. They were the first to outline freedom and equality as social values in similar terms as we know them in our time. However, freedom and equality were preserved for Athenians, free men with properties, who had plenty of spare time as they didn't have to worry about their survival supplies. That's perhaps a significant difference between Athenians and you, but here comes the most interesting issue about stoicism: It emerged in a slave-based society and it was created to be suitable for everybody: slaves and emperors.

Athenians, released from the daily duty of earning a living, spent lots of time in public spaces, dedicating themselves to political debates in the Agora and reflecting on life (Mark, 2021). Since they were not worried about how to expand their business, philosophy was a frequent activity, accessible around the corner.

Philosophy in the Hellenistic civilization initiated a way to think and explain reality, and settled the basis of the intellectual tradition for what we call *Western civilization.* The search for a rational explanation for everything that surrounds us and the need to have an understanding of life, the universe, and fate was first addressed by the Hellenists. The fields they focused on were physics, to understand nature and how everything follows an invariable pattern; logic, covering not only the evident relationship among things or ideas but also a reflection on the language and how people can learn about reality, and develop acknowledgment; and ethics, tightly related to logic, as the search for the best life for human beings (Internet Encyclopedia of Philosophy, n.d.).

After over two thousand years of philosophers' thinking, all these matters might seem insignificant: They must have found all the answers we need. However, if you reread the last paragraph, those questions still underlie our lives: Why do things happen in this or that way? What can I do about it? How can I build a better life for myself, and for those who I love? What is the best I can get?

By now, you might be wondering how the answers that former Stoics found to these questions in such a different society from ours could be useful nowadays. Let's begin with the story of the father of stoicism, Zeno. It could be anyone's story.

According to Zeno's biographer, Diogenes Laertius, he wasn't born in Hellenistic lands. Zeno was called *"the Phoenician."* The Phoenicians were people who founded harbor cities and traded along the Mediterranean shores. Zeno was one of them and had traveled a lot as a merchant, and came over to Hellenist cities frequently. On some of his many visits to Athens, he heard about philosophers that were so common there (Einzelgänger, 2020).

Although he was captivated by philosophy and wanted to learn more about what Socrates and Plato were teaching, Zeno had a very busy, practical life: He had to get his ship ready to sail, count and control his commodities, and be aware of his profit and losses. Zeno had inherited his father's business and was a very successful merchant, carrying and selling goods in the most important commercial centers. However, his life took an unexpected turn.

When he was still very young, a storm took Zeno unaware while he was sailing toward Athens with a significant shipment. The wind and the violent waves ended in Zeno being shipwrecked somewhere close to the shores of Athens. Although his life was saved, Zeno witnessed how all his father's and his life's efforts and achievements were swallowed by the sea. Within a few hours, everything he had disappeared (Let's talk about philosophy, 2019). He reached the coast and entered Athens as a despondent and hopeless man.

How would you feel if, after years of hard work, everything you've earned is lost due to the strength of nature? How many people have seen their business drown for unexpected causes? What are your options when destiny plays that rudely with you?

Once in Athens, Zeno had his first encounter with philosophers and began learning about some of their lessons. After some time hearing about Xenophon, Socrates, and Plato's ideas, he said: *I made a prosperous voyage when I was shipwrecked* (Let's talk about philosophy, 2019). In the worst circumstances, Zeno found the possibility to earn a new perspective on life. He realized that, after all, he hadn't lost *everything* he had. It sounds easy, but it isn't. It's simple.

Zeno started reading the most relevant philosophy books of the time and learned from the philosophers that taught in public places in Athens. Living as an Athenian, Zeno observed that most people in the city lived unhappily, desiring what they didn't have and worrying about losing what they had. Since he had lost all the material things he owned himself and through philosophy, could see things from a different perspective, he searched to convey a more permanent value that could replace pleasure, which was Athenians' most common concern (Mark, 2011). That's when Zeno decided to share and teach his ideas and created the Stoic School.

The word *stoicism* derives from a Greek architectural element, the *stoa*. This was a covered walkway that served as a public space for different activities for everyday people, such as a marketplace, an informal gallery where artists could display their artwork, and even a space for religious gatherings. The *stoa* was also the place where Zeno and his followers would meet to discuss philosophy. This is how the concept of stoicism came to be known as *The Philosophy of The Porch*.

Zeno started his "school" in a place accessible for anyone to listen, learn, participate, and discuss. Plato created the Academy, and later Aristotle, his Lyceum, to give their pupils lessons, but both were located outside the fortified city. Instead, Zeno wanted to remain in direct contact with the Athenians. He wanted to be close to people as his philosophy was meant to serve the common and everyday person's needs.

This could be the main factor that contributed to making stoicism the most influential philosophy of the Hellenistic age. The school never set a fixed place, but rather moved through Athens, and even ended up being taught in gymnasiums and music halls. (Wycherley, 1978).

Enduring Over Two Thousand Years: A Bit of History

It may be argued that one of the main reasons Stoicism has endured for over two thousand years is due to the Roman empire, and the incorporation of this philosophy into its culture. Between 200 and 100 BCE, the Romans, still as a Republic, continued to expand their domains, reaching the Macedonian empire. With Alexander the Great, all the Hellenistic cities had fallen under this new empire that had unified the territories and extended their power to the limits of the Ganges river in India. After Alexander's death, the Macedonian empire was impaired and was unable to oppose the Roman powerful armies. Then, the Romans occupied and dominated all that had once been Alexander's reign (Kane, 2018).

The Romans appropriated a lot of Greek culture, including their philosophical ideas. Stoicism became very popular in Rome, although it was adapted to the particular nuances of Roman society. This adapted version of Stoicism aligned very well with important Roman customs, such as *self-discipline* and *gravitas.* This concept referred to not being ruled by shameful or inappropriate emotions. Finally, the concept of *loyalty* to Rome was a key aspect of this society. Marcus Aurelius, known as the Stoic Roman Emperor, strived to apply a Stoic mentality throughout his lifetime.

In the 4th century, the Roman Empire embraced Christianity. After centuries of persecution of Christ's parishioners, this new religion became a resource to consolidate the internal stability of the state. For the Roman emperors, it was possible to establish Christianity as the new official religion of the empire because many of its fundamentals were already rooted in people's mindsets. Stoicism somehow led the way for Christianity (Smiley, 1934).

Christianity is the funnel that brought stoicism through the Middle Ages into the Modern era until the Renaissance and later the Enlightenment. These two ideological currents retrieved Greek and Roman philosophers from the Classical period, including stoicism. Although Stoic texts were not widely read in the 19th century, it was revitalized in the 1900s.

There is a historical thread that links our contemporary societies to Ancient Greece and Rome and Christianity. Our vision of life has been shaped by these two strong paradigms that have been synthesized at some points (Stanford Encyclopedia of Philosophy, 2023). The whole history of Europe is entrenched in the evolution of societies over what once was the Roman Empire, with Christianity as the official religion. Later, Europeans spread their culture to the rest of the globe. The fundamental principle and values outlined by this heritage have been able to survive the political and economic revolutions and crises, and the accelerated rhythm of progress. Standing at the beginning of the new millennium, stoicism still makes sense to us because these cultural nuances are written in our social DNA.

The Evolution of Stoicism—From Ancient to Contemporary Society

Like many other philosophical currents, stoicism has passed through different spreading waves. Every time, those waves were tightly associated with cultural and social transformations that made stoicism principles relevant again adapted to new contexts. What happened to western societies in the last two thousand years that brought this system of ideas to our days? How can stoicism help us in our present?

Stoicism has been able to survive because it is based on two basic principles that rely on human nature: People have the power to accept and the power to control. People throughout history, including you, have had similar issues to deal with: the need to survive, the anguish of losing those you love, the frustration of not achieving your goals, or being unable to change the life you have, among others.

After losing everything, Zeno arrived at a first conclusion: You might not have the power to control what happens, but you can control how it affects you (Aperture, 2021). This simple and powerful statement provides the basis for stoicism, back in Zeno's times, and still in our current everyday life.

This approach has been able to survive by interpreting and adapting to different social contexts. Most of the teachings of the original Stoics were never written; they were oral discourses, which followers or acquaintances would later materialize into paper. The few examples of original Stoic thoughts recorded by themselves can be found in Seneca's letters to friends, family, and apprentices. Another valuable source of the former Stoics' thoughts is the famous personal journal of emperor Marcus Aurelius. However, he never intended for this journal to become accessible to the public, as it was a personal conversation with himself about the struggles, sense of duty, musings, and reminders of what it meant to be a Stoic, an emperor, a man of service, a Roman who lived in harmony with nature and himself and honored the gods.

The texts and lessons taught by the original Stoics are available today due to the work of preservation carried out by the different followers of the philosophers. During the Renaissance, stoicism was read and used to understand all the transformations that occurred: The Black Death, the Protestant Reformation, the Counter Reformation, and economic changes due to the revitalization of commerce. All these processes led to deep social transformation, putting common sense and collective beliefs in parentheses. Philosophers were searching for a new way to build social peace and political restoration. Later, classical philosophers considered aligned Christian ideas to be associated with truth. Therefore, stoicism was taken as a philosophy that helped people to find the truth and seek the good in the middle of a tempestuous world (Daily Stoic, n.d.).

At the end of the 17th century, Baruch Spinoza developed a new system of ideas that combined modern ideas about science and rationality with ancient principles of stoicism, building a bridge between this classical system of ideas and the Enlightenment (Stanford Encyclopedia of Philosophy, 2020). He searched for a new way to understand life in a more joyful manner, in harmony with the cosmos (Pursuit of Wonder, 2022). Influenced by stoicism, Spinoza thought that our happiness and well-being didn't depend on our passions and the ordinary needs we usually search for (Stanford Encyclopedia of Philosophy, 2020). Reason becomes a tool that supports our will, and helps us gain control over our emotions. The central role of reason and its potential to control not only emotions but also nature was reinforced by Positivism in the following centuries.

The 20th century was described by the historian Eric Hobsbawm as the Age of Catastrophes (Hobsbawm, 1995). The Modern concept of indefinite progress was challenged by all the destruction that scientific and technological development brought. Wars, diseases, casualties, nothing of that was supposed to be the consequence of the efforts the Positivists made in the 19th century. The world was expected to follow a path of unlimited prosperity that would reach every person. Instead, there was tragedy, suffering, and a deep disenchantment.

Philosophy, as a reflection of society, stopped searching for truth and absolute certainties. People had new concerns, and that reflected on philosophical currents. The general ambitious goals of humankind that characterized modernity were replaced by the individual and introspective search for inner calm. Perhaps this was a way to survive in a world that was falling apart.

Stoicism taught in the past how to avoid everything surrounding you that could affect you. Happiness was no longer something you would find outside. The new millennium has put new challenges to people, and once again, stoicism can provide useful tools to find equilibrium.

Human beings have a natural inclination to search for goods and success as a means to achieve happiness. Nowadays, those goals are somewhat easier to meet, and many people have wealthy and prosperous careers but yet, do not feel happy or fulfilled. There is a sense of existential emptiness related to the disappearance of the traditional idea of happiness. The idea of having it all, when *all* can be rendered as material stuff, succeeding according to external parameters fixed by others, to meet others' expectations, doesn't seem to be valid anymore. One of the most remarkable Stoics, Seneca, taught at his times that power and wealth don't make a person happy by themselves: There is something more needed. That's what stoicism helps to find (Daily Stoic, n.d.).

Chapter 2:

Stoic Principles and Key Virtues

What would you answer if someone asked you some of these questions: *What's your purpose in life? Why do you study, work, and have relationships? What do you search for?* You would probably answer that all you want in life is to be happy. Everything you do is to achieve happiness. All the rest—money, success, a family, prestige—is just a means to accomplish that major goal. We can assume that this is an innate trait of human nature. People might find different things that make them happy, but that is one thing they have in common with a hunter in the Paleolithic, a peasant in the Middle Ages, and a merchant in the Modern era. Who doesn't want to be happy?

Stoicism, like most of the philosophy schools in Ancient Greece, searched for happiness. It was called *eudaimonia.* The term is more accurately translated as "human flourishing," but for understanding, we can use happiness as the essential meaning. For Stoics, the seeking of *eudaimonia* was directly linked with ethics, the reflection on what is good or wrong. Therefore, there is a necessary correspondence between what is considered virtuous—what is good—and happiness. Seeking happiness was the same thing as the search for virtuous behavior. There could be no contradiction. This is absolutely relevant to understand why being happy was so important: There is no good without happiness. Human dignity could not flourish if people were incapable of experiencing happiness (Garrett, 2021).

In this search for virtue through happiness, stoicism proposes a particular approach to what happens around us and to us, and how to react in front of that. Stoicism is the art of letting go of overly emotional reactions, relying on a logical and rational mindset, and the practical application of habits and tools. The key is to be able to keep calm, understand the new conditions and make new decisions to act. It is pointless to feel sorry, find the one to blame, and think about how it could have been avoided. It just doesn't matter anymore because what has happened is already in the past, and the past cannot be changed. Instead of crying or releasing our rage, or letting ourselves be dragged into frustration, stoicism proposes different ways to face adversity.

It doesn't only apply when a terrible tragedy comes to our lives, as it happened to Zeno. We constantly face challenging situations in our daily life and even if they aren't making us bankrupt or putting us in terrible danger, they upset us, and make us feel miserable. Stoicism is not a philosophy to turn to when you feel at the edge. Instead, it helps you live intensely and happily every day of your life. We shall see in the following chapters why stoicism pays so much attention to everyday life, and how you can acquire the Stoic mindset to live in accordance with that. It is so much worth it!

When the word *stoicism* or *Stoic* philosophy appears, people frequently tend to assume its core belief is that of rejecting, ignoring, or even denying emotions. Nothing is further from the truth than those assumptions! Stoicism promotes a new attitude placed on a rational and logical basis above all, even emotions, not to neglect but to link them to more realistic stimuli and outcomes. One of the purposes of this book is to clarify these principles that have usually been misunderstood.

There is a lot of confusion about this Stoic principle of not letting things affect you and being happy despite all of it. It is commonly related to indifference, or a secret ability to repress emotions. Stoicism detractors claim that stoicism is about imposing rationality over feelings, leaving, as a result, insensitive people. Nonetheless, placing reason before emotions can be understood in two ways: either you neglect and repress your emotions, or you struggle to deliberately dominate them. Stoicism is more profound than that. It proposes an approach to seeing the world and understanding life and promotes a way to be in the world and experience your life. It is not about turning unemotional. Stoicism is a deeply humanistic philosophical stance.

The Four Key Virtues of Stoicism

Before delving into the key virtues of stoicism, let's clarify the concept of virtue. Being virtuous is not exactly the same as being good. While good or bad are attributes, virtue is an attitude developed by habits. Ancient Greeks had the term *arete* to define virtue. This can be explained as a state of character that leads people to meet their real essence as human beings. Stoics based their conception of the *arete* on Aristotle's idea about humankind: We are both rational and social. Therefore, to be virtuous, we need to behave rationally and cooperate socially (Garrett, 2021). Virtue as a whole is the level of perfection of human rationality.

For most ancient philosophical schools, virtue equals good, and eudaimonia (happiness). There is no possible contradiction between them. For Stoics, everything that tears you apart from the search for virtue must be ignored and avoided. At the same time, things that might seem negative at first such as suffering or tragedies, don't have the power to affect you because they are external, so they don't interfere between you and virtue.

There are four main virtues that Stoics invite you to enhance:

Prudence

The Greek term is *phronesis*, also rendered as "wisdom" (Hanselman, n.d.). This virtue replaces a lot of undesirable emotions and pointless feelings that might make you feel overwhelmed: overthinking, anxiety, and fear, just to name a few. It implies a rational awareness of what you can do and a reflection on why you should or shouldn't do it considering the consequences which are not under your control. To act in the right way is the wise way to act (Bele, 2021).

Prudence compels you to ask yourself before acting: *Why am I doing this? What if I didn't do it?* People are constantly dragged into a frenetic routine and it seems impossible to reflect on every action before taking it. Nonetheless, this previous moment of reflection can be trained and incorporated as a habit. Once you learn to live your life in correspondence with the Stoic principles, you develop a new awareness of yourself and a different perception of time and urgency.

Temperance

Stoics talk about *sophrosyne*: self-control (Hanselman, n.d.). It is about gaining control over your actions and being capable of deciding what deserves to be done, and what can be avoided; deciphering what you can do given your abilities or the circumstances, and accepting what you can't do. Imagine how much your levels of pressure and frustration can diminish if you could just focus your energy on what is worth it (Bele, 2021). Since stoicism is deeply rational, the power of temperance prevents you from being towed by passions and acting impulsively.

Temperance demands a process of self-awareness, learning about yourself, what your abilities and strengths are, and admitting your weaknesses and limitations. This way, you will have rational arguments to decide on before acting.

At the same time, the development of temperance also requires a broad understanding of nature and a conscious analysis of your circumstances. This is key to recognizing the external determinants that impose conditions on your actions.

Courage

Stoics retrieve Aristotle's lessons about the search for virtue. The main goal is to find the golden mean: Neither coward nor reckless, brave (Diaz, 2020). Being courageous doesn't mean searching for danger or taking hazardous situations just as they come. That would be irrational. Instead, courage implies being ready to face life's many and constant challenges.

Human beings have a natural tilt to wish for good. We expect good things to happen and be lucky enough to dodge tragedy. Obvious as it sounds, this is yet impossible. Life is full of challenges and painful events you will eventually find in your lane. Courage is precisely about being ready to face them. Since Stoics don't promote anticipating the future and worrying about it because it is beyond your control, they foster you to be courageous instead. No matter what may come, you will have the strength to deal with it (Bele, 2021).

Stoics also believe that people have all the resources needed to thrive. Nature has been wise enough to equip you with the required strengths and skills that are already inside you. It just takes a personal inner journey to unlock them.

Justice

We can find different conceptions about what is considered just. For Stoics, it implies giving each person what is due, what they deserve. In the same sense, it is about recognizing the accurate measure of the importance of any situation: no more and no less. Even though it sounds simple, it isn't easy to deliver justice. It isn't limited to behaving in accordance with the law. It is a personal disposition to rational judgment about ourselves and everything around us. It demands the sum of all the other three virtues.

Stoics consider that a natural and harmonic order determines the proportions: There is enough of anything for everybody and the right amount for each. Individual ethical behavior connotes noticing those proportions and acting with respect (Bele, 2021). Stoicism set other essential virtues under the umbrella of justice: kindness, cooperation, honesty, and piety concerning their religious beliefs (Hanselman, n.d.).

You aren't meant just to bear life and survive, or lodge your happiness in what is ephemeral. You are meant to thrive. Virtue is the only path to thoroughly display your human condition. This is a new concept of success and a sense of purpose.

The Principles of Stoicism

To refer to the core principles of stoicism, we can't turn back to one systematized writing that summarizes them. Stoics' ideas have reached us through fragments of writings of some of the most remarkable figures, and other less-known Stoic philosophers. However, it is possible to identify the main concepts taught by Zeno and his disciples.

Former Stoic philosophy comprised reflection and study in three realms: physics, regarding nature; logic, considering the rational order beyond everything that exists; and ethics, as the reflection on good and evil that guide our acts. To Stoics, the three of them were interconnected and represented a whole (Stanford Encyclopedia of Philosophy, 2023). These pillars can be disaggregated into the following principles.

Happiness is Found in Virtue

People search for happiness by pursuing things. Stoics think that this is a wrong assumption: There is no possible way to achieve happiness but by being virtuous. In the previous section, we explored the Stoics' conception of virtue.

First of all, the Stoics didn't conceive that anything could be more important than virtue. Our essence as human beings needs to keep aligned with the rest of the universe, in constant pursuit of the good. Good equals happiness. The common belief of happiness embodied in external things takes it out of your control. If you depend on external things to feel good, it will make you weak and dependent on external issues. The virtuous person is also free; hence, they can't be determined by what they have or not, what they gain or lose.

Many toxic emotions you are probably familiar with are rooted in this mistaken conception of how to be happy. Anxiety, fear, frustration, and despair are all consequences of the things we need, cherish, and don't want to miss (Garrett, 2021).

Everything Is Ordered According to Reason

Stoics believed that everything in the universe, including the human condition, follows a natural order established by reason. Therefore, it can be intelligible: Everything has an explanation based on reason.

This principle has a direct relationship with freedom and will. You can truly be free because you have the capacity to understand what happens around you. Then, you act according to reasoned decisions. Sometimes circumstances hasten our reactions instead of being aware of what we want to do, or what would be the best to do. No matter what external events or things tell you, you always have a *reasoned choice*, and that is what you should focus on (Hanselman, n.d.). The reasoned choice, then, is the always-existing option to deliberately decide what to do, or not to do.

Live in Harmony With Nature

Stoics believed that everything that exists is interconnected. Our personal lives are linked to all other living organisms and the universe. Anything that happens can impact us in ways we might not even notice, and yet they can bring us good or cause harm. At the same time, every connection in the universe has a purpose; every little thing has a reason to exist and altogether creates a coherent whole. You, as an individual, are a tiny part of that whole, still with your own purpose (Hanselman, n.d.).

The advice of living in harmony with nature implies understanding that there is an order, a pattern, a path traced beyond your power. It is pointless to fight against it. Let's see an easy example: In winter, it is usual that days are cold, and it snows. Instead of expecting sunny days or longing for the summer, grab some wooden sticks for the stove!

These ideas led Stoics to dedicate themselves to studying physics: The better they could understand nature, the more prepared they would be to learn the reasons behind it and be able to recognize the reasoned choice.

The Attitude of Indifference

Stoicism is usually associated with the idea of indifference. This is, in part, true. Stoics promote an attitude toward all external things that imply indifference. If individuals are meant to pursue happiness only by virtue, all the other things should be ignored or not given too much attention. What happens with the people you love? What about your personal goals and accomplishments? Don't they deserve to be cherished and valued?

Of course, it's not that simple. Although Stoics consider that those externals distract you from your search for virtue, they wouldn't advise you to stop feeling or avoiding emotions. In preference, those customary issues you care about should be perceived as worthy but not considered ultimate ends (Garrett, 2021).

Focus on What You Can Control

Stoicism is a consistent approach; therefore, each idea is closely linked to the others. In this sense, Stoics believed that all things that fall beyond your control don't deserve attention. If you can't control them, then just pass on them.

Of course, some duties and commitments are still important to you. Zeno taught that there are *"preferred and dispreferred indifferents"* (Hanselman, n.d.). Externals have different values assigned by you; some of them will accompany you on the path of virtue while others won't. You need to establish your priorities and focus on what you can effectively control.

There are just a few things you can actually control: Your own thoughts, opinions, and decisions. Everything exceeding this is considered external. When you learn to leave externals aside, you gain steadiness (*eustatheia*) since you live in harmony with nature—don't fight the inevitable—and base your decisions on reason—the reasoned choice (Hanselman, n.d.). While it might sound selfish, it is in fact, a responsible way to assume responsibilities: you commit to doing just what really is within your reach.

Stoics Search for "Eupatheia"

This word indicates good passions and emotions and is opposed to negative emotions such as fear, anger, and anxiety, which should be avoided. Stoics consider that reason is always behind emotions, therefore it is possible—through conscious processes—to prioritize good emotions over the negative (Holiday & Hanselman, n.d.).

Three positive emotions lead to *eupatheia*: joy, caution, and wishing. All of them result from rational actions. For example, caution is defined as a rational avoidance of what might harm you (Holiday & Hanselman, n.d.). This eliminates or diminishes fear from your life and replaces hope. Hope is not positive thinking as it implies projecting into the future, expecting what you can't control (Hanselman, n.d.). In the end, it just triggers anxiety and eventually, fear.

Everything Flows and Changes

We have already seen that one of the core principles of stoicism is to live in harmony with nature and that everything is already naturally ordered. The next important thing about this is that this order isn't static but fluid. Things change constantly. That's the fact. You might have heard about this quote attributed to Heraclitus "No man ever steps in the same river twice. For it's not the same river, and he's not the same man" (Desautels, 2018).

As Stoics invite you to accept what is destined to be, since it is determined by a natural purpose, they also prompt you to accept that nothing remains invariant. Then, you shouldn't be either. You need to flow with the stream. What causes you pain today will be gone tomorrow. What gives you pleasure now won't last forever. The sooner you learn to accept these facts, the less likely you are to suffer.

There Is No Good or Evil

We have already mentioned that one of the three pillars of the Stoic philosophy is ethics, a reflection of what is good and evil. Stoicism asserts that these aren't intrinsic attributes of things. It is a matter of perspective. If everything has been ordered by nature and there is a purpose in it, then it can't be intrinsically wrong. What you decide about externals concerning your search for happiness determines if it is good or bad (Hanselman, n.d.).

Just as happiness can't be separated from virtue, good is linked to reason. Toxic emotions are just externals that don't result from reasoned choices. It is your judgment that will create good. However, there is still an ethical principle beyond this one: You are compelled to decide and do the best you can.

Sense of Duty

Although stoicism promotes an attitude of indifference, it doesn't imply negligence or indolence. On the contrary, as a humanistic approach, stoicism believes in a deep sense of a unified self. You, like every other individual, are a part of the perfect order of nature and are interconnected to all the rest of beings. You must assume full responsibility for this but, unlike what we tend to do, it doesn't come from external commitments.

Since reasoned choice empowers you to act freely and always according to your own will, and you aren't expected to act over things beyond your control, then there is no one else left to blame by yourself. This is, in fact, a practical ethical behavior. Externals won't affect you, therefore you can't charge for them.

This ethical dimension of stoicism proves the assumption on this philosophy promoting selfishness wrong. People with an internally based sense of duty are totally aligned with the common good. The golden rule of Stoics is *'No man is an island'* (Hanselman, n.d.). Each of us acting in correspondence to reason and searching for virtue eventually results in virtuous and harmonic societies.

The Art of Understanding What You Can Control and What You Can't

So far, you might have noticed that besides the coherent development of concepts that stoicism comprises, there is a practical dimension to each of the ideas. Virtues shouldn't be perceived as abstract distant goals. Instead, they are habits that can be grabbed with a bit of effort. Remember what the Stoics said: Inside yourself, you will find all the resources you need to display the perfection of human rationality. It is just part of your essence.

Learning about Stoic principles helps us understand why it is possible to develop those virtues and achieve happiness. There are simple questions you can ask yourself to begin:

- Do you take your time to think before making decisions?
- How do you decide your goals?
- What determines your duties?
- How do you react to things you can't control?
- Are you able to decide to let things go if they are too complicated or bring you negative emotions?
- Are you being controlled by the desire for pleasure?
- Are you being controlled by the fear of pain or suffering?
- What do you do when circumstances don't favor you?

The list isn't limited to these as they are just starting points. You will find more questions to ask yourself as you progress in finding these answers.

Human Virtue Is Based on Striving for Excellence

If there is one statement to remember about stoicism, it's this one: Human beings are destined to embody the perfection of rationality. Therefore, they are condemned to cultivate virtue and achieve excellence. There is no other purpose in life, whether you are already aware of it or not.

Some people would say that having excellence as the main goal puts too much pressure on them. Isn't stoicism about moving smoothly through life, adapting to constant change, and accepting the imponderables? Stoicism will answer that excellence is exactly about that. You shouldn't expect happiness from money, your relationships with others, success, or even health. All those are externals that can—and will—change from one moment to another. Excellence equals virtue, and virtue implies discerning what matters and what doesn't.

At this point, it is important to highlight that stoicism is a way of life, not a goal. The emphasis is on the process instead of the result. One of the main aphorisms of stoicism is 'persist and resist'. We are habituated to evaluating what we do or want in terms of results: *If I get this or that, I will be happier*; *If I earn more or buy stuff, I will feel more fulfilled*. Have you ever wondered how you felt while you were pursuing those goals? Were you aware of happiness when you achieved them? How many times do you complain about all the bad things that happen that stop you from being happy? The key is the process.

Stoicism represents a major change in your life, in your perception of yourself and everything around you. Being simple is one of the most difficult tasks. Nonetheless, stoicism also teaches that every little step you take has a powerful cascading effect. It is important to exercise preferred and dispreferred indifference because minor concerns trigger negative emotions that deviate from the pursuit of virtue. In the opposite sense, every little battle you win has long-term positive impacts, even if you don't notice them at first sight.

Human nature is meant to thrive for excellence. You just need to learn to flow with the stream.

Chapter 3:

From Slaves to Emperors

Stoicism is a philosophy suitable for everybody, from slaves to emperors, in Ancient Greece and contemporary cities. All the principles and the former virtues of stoicism described in the previous chapter were outlined by the founders of Stoicism as a philosophical school. More than two millennia later, they still make sense to us since they are based on the most elementary basis of our human nature.

This chapter intends to reflect on how stoicism became an applicable philosophy for everyday people, even at its former stage. Although we won't cover all the principal characters of the school, we shall delve into the life and ideas of some of the most remarkable Stoics, in particular in the classical period. This will reaffirm why stoicism is a philosophy for slaves as well as for emperors.

Stoicism's most important characters belonged to different social segments. We have chosen four of the former philosophers that laid stoicism foundations: Zeno, Epictetus, Seneca, and Marcus Aurelius. A merchant, a slave, a senator, and an emperor.

A Merchant: Zeno of Citium

Although he was the founder of the Stoic school of philosophy in Athens, he was a foreigner. In ancient Greece, those born in other *polis* (cities that were autonomous states) were considered *metics*. Like Zeno, most *metics* came to Athens as traders. They didn't have the same civil rights as the Athenian citizens, for instance, they couldn't acquire lands or participate in political life (Jones, 2015).

Zeno was born in Citium, Cyprus, in 336–265 BCE. He became a merchant, inheriting his father's business. He was only 22 years old when the unexpected happened: He was shipwrecked on the shore of Athens, losing everything he had. This was the moment when he decided to leave his life as a sailor and a merchant and dedicate himself to teaching philosophy. What led him to that decision? During his trips, he read Xenophon's *Memorabilia* and heard about Socrates' ideas. Later, he followed Crates of Thebes and other philosophers. From them, he learned the first ideas that would help him to accept his new living conditions (Mark, 2011).

At the age of 35, after a while of living as an Athenian, he started his own school retrieving some of his teachers' ideas. One of the first lessons he learned from them was about one of the most common faults that besieged people: to say yes to everything instantaneously (Let's talk philosophy, 2019). How often do you say *yes*?

We don't know if he chose the *stoa*, the gate of the marketplace, because that's where he felt more at home, or because it was one of the most crowded places in the Agora. For sure, that was the place where Zeno could talk to common people while they were engaged in their ordinary activities. It was there where everyday life occurred.

Zeno never systematized his ideas or left writings with his teachings. Instead, most of his philosophy reaches us through his disciples and his biographer, Diogenes Laertius (Mark, 2011). His main concern, as a man of his time, was how to help people achieve happiness. Let's try to imagine Zeno after his tragedy trying to find an answer to that question: How can I be happy? It is not difficult to understand why he needed to search for happiness in something else but material things. Then, he concluded that "Instead of pleasure, one should court reason and recognize that all things are impermanent and without lasting value" (Mark, 2011, para 9).

Progressively, Zeno continued to develop his reasoning about why pleasure made people slaves of their passions and eventually led them to sorrow. Through an understanding of natural order and nurturing self-awareness, it was possible to get rid of all the superfluous needs. He established that at the heart of stoicism is the constant search to live in harmony with nature. He called this *euroia biou*—which can be translated to the literal words "euphoria of life," or "smooth flow of life." According to Zeno, circumstances compel you to behave in a certain way, and even if you intend to resist, it is still the only option. We might call it fate; Zeno just believed that reality flows and changes, and the sooner you learn what you can control and what you cannot, the better for you to make accurate decisions (Let's talk philosophy, 2019).

On another hand, understanding human nature implied learning Aristotle's teachings: We are social animals, and we're capable of reasoning. Nevertheless, we do not do it *all* the time. Although we constantly fall down to our emotions, Zeno affirmed that reason released people from what oppressed them. Emotions are mere information about the outside world, but never the protagonists of any situation.

The training of one's mind to prepare oneself for any challenge, and realize that emotions are only there to help is actually the means to the greatest end: living a virtuous life. So, the true purpose of stoicism isn't to train people to become emotionless, unable to react to anything or experience any feeling. Its true purpose is a way of life that focuses on what really matters—the imperishable. It intends to emphasize that at the end of the day, humans are mortal, and life is greater than struggles. Why would you spend a lifetime fretting over situations you can't control?

Interestingly, Zeno reasoned that the source of human misery came from disconnection or detachment from one's purpose, from a connection to others, and the natural environment. The key to connecting your purpose to the natural order is self-awareness, and through this, becoming aware of others and everything surrounding you. It gives you the ability to achieve *eudaimonia* by living in correspondence with the flow of life (Let's talk philosophy, 2019). You need to strengthen the capacity to 'read' the *logos*, the reason beyond the universe that outlines your destiny, and just accept and adapt to it. On the contrary, by focusing on what disturbed it—the *pathos* or emotions—you would be giving up living a virtuous and happy life.

It mustn't have been easy for Zeno to flow with the stream after finding himself alone, in a city where he would never be considered a citizen and therefore, would never enjoy full rights. He was a young *metic* who had lost his wealth and had no prestige. He had to build his life from the ashes. Nature had taken all he had; there is nothing he could have done to avoid being shipwrecked. He couldn't blame himself for being doomed to poverty. Instead of remorse or a sense of failure, he cultivated a new system of ideas to face this challenge that life presented to him.

One of the most powerful messages Stoics convey is that, as a philosophical stance, it didn't result from mere intellectual reflection. It is the practical response to real experiences. Zeno developed this system of ideas to overcome his own tragedy and move forward. Against all odds, Zeno wasn't only able to do that, but also to create one of the most influential philosophical schools of all time. Don't you wonder how a person that has nothing could think about helping others?

Like Zeno, we believe that we are destined to thrive through collective purpose, since it is the same image of our own purpose. And like Zeno was, ready to cooperate with others and share his wisdom, we intend to share his teachings with you. Stoicism motivates us to flourish with others.

A Slave: Epictetus

Epictetus was born in 55 in Greece when it belonged to the Roman Empire. By that time, Nero was the emperor. There is no historical evidence of his real name. Nero was the name he was known by. In Greek, "Epictetus" means acquired. He was taken from his hometown and taken to Rome as a slave. He was the property of one of Nero's administrators (Dobbin & Graver, 2021).

Slaves in Roman society were not considered people. Metics had no civil rights in Ancient Athens, but they were still respected as human beings. Slaves, instead, were considered goods, property that their owners could buy, sell, torture, and even kill. Although Epictetus belonged to an important man and wasn't forced to bond labor, he used to be tortured. On one occasion, his tormentor broke his leg (Mr. Smart, 2020a).

Enduring the hardships of slavery, he managed to attend lectures by Stoic philosopher Musonius Rufus. Later, he was allowed to buy his freedom when Nero died. Then, Epictetus founded his own school to teach stoicism. Nonetheless, after 25 years of teaching in Rome, he was compelled to leave. He returned to Greece and settled in Nicopolis (Dobbin & Graver, 2021). His experience as a slave forged his character, based on patience and tolerance. Stoicism gave him the tools to avoid external circumstances, defining who he was and aiming to become. He had to cope with uprooting twice, physical mistreatment that left him lame and dealing with the stigma of being a liberated slave for the rest of his life. All the pain he came through gained him the epithet of the *Prophet of Endurance* (Mr. Smart, 2020a).

His lessons were compiled in the *Discourses*, but they weren't written by himself. His ideas were retrieved by his students and this book was ghostwritten by Arrian of Nicomedia. The *Encheiridion*, which means Manual or Handbook, is a summarized version of the Discourses that allows us to approach Epictetus's thoughts. Arrian included not only Epictetus' lectures but also the students' discussions. The main concern was how to live life as Stoics. Although most of Epictetus's students were high-class Romans, the issues they were interested in could be anybody's. They talked about profound topics and the deepest purpose in life, but also ordinary issues that involved relationships, wealth and poverty, and how to be a good citizen.

Epictetus, a good Stoic, searched for understanding and self-awareness, but with a strong basis in experience. To him, philosophy should be applied to daily life. He was a pragmatic man and recommended to be always proactive, no matter what the circumstances or who the people involved were. He insisted that individuals are a result of their decisions, and not of their conditions. While being permanently surrounded by struggles that awaken anger, frustration, and unhappiness, letting those emotions grow just lead you to more and more pain.

You constantly face situations that trigger rage and irritation for things that you can't control. Those feelings won't make you any happier.

Let's think about an example of a situation Epictetus might have lived in. In Ancient Rome, it was a popular activity to visit public baths. There, the pleasure of bathing in warm waters coexisted with the discomfort of being in a place full of people, having to wait for your turn, and dealing with others' unpleasant behaviors. It made no sense to get angry about that. In such a dilemma, you would have two options: You don't go and miss the enjoyment of the baths, or you accept what it takes and have some fun. Now, try to think about your daily life: You have to wait for your turn at the cafeteria and end up spending almost all your lunch break waiting in line. How does getting angry help you feel better? Simple. It doesn't.

Being proactive comes along with becoming accountable for your decisions. You have to take responsibility for your actions. If your happiness doesn't depend on others, nobody can be blamed for your actions. Responsibility can be split into two words to understand the concept: response-ability, the ability to be accountable for your responses (Mr. Smart, 2020a). Epictetus said: "It is not enough to be hit or insulted to be harmed, you must believe you're being harmed. If someone succeeds in provoking you, you realize your mind is complicit in the provocation" (Bertoloti, 2022, para 8).

Epictetus knew that everything takes time and has a process to evolve. If you think just about the ultimate goal, you will probably feel frustrated. Instead, if you are well aware of what it takes, you will develop patience and work to carry on the process. The human mind doesn't fruit quickly or easily. Do you remember how we started exploring stoicism? We started with the idea of stoicism being simple, but not easy.

Whatever you choose to be or do in your life, it will have some obstacles to overcome; there will be some losses before you finally achieve success. It will be a process with interruptions. Don't let them deviate your attention. Put your efforts and direct your energy to what you can control and get ready to let go of the things you don't.

There is a limited list of issues that completely fall under our control: our opinions, ideas, aversions, and wishes. That is what we can decide through reason. Anything else is beyond the borders, even our own bodies. Illnesses or accidents can happen and how our physical body reacts is not our decision. Even further out of reach, there are other people's opinions, and social evaluations, even about ourselves, our possessions, and what others do. That shouldn't be of our concern.

Epictetus made a distinction:

- Internal: how we respond to what happens to us.

- External: what happens to us.

Our problems result from a lack of ability to distinguish between both groups. Instead of wishing things to happen as you want, accept the way things happen the way they do (Mr. Smart, 2020b).

Besides this distinction between externals and internals, Epictetus identified three *topoi* that represented three disciplines to dominate. The first *topoi* are composed of desires and aversions: They are the sources of emotions that blur the ability to behave in accordance with reason. The discipline of desire implies not desiring what you can't earn by yourself. You can't wish to have the power to fly; you can wish to learn how to fly a plane, only if you act in consequence and take classes. Otherwise, you will lead yourself to frustration.

The second *topoi* is *reacting* versus *acting* deliberately in correspondence to duty which implies avoiding acting carelessly. We have previously discussed the attitude of indifference that Stoics promote and how a wrong comprehension of that has conducted others to misinterpret stoicism as an indolent or selfish set of values. Stoicism has an intense sense of commitment to others. Acting always implies the previous reflection on the reasons beyond the act and not only the consequences. It covers the discipline of action: Behave to accomplish our role within society referring to our relationships: The family, the workplace, and the community.

The final *topoi* are freedom from deception and composure, everything that falls within the area of judgment. It takes developing the discipline of assent: The act of deciding the way you think about what something is. The moment to affirm you approve or agree to a certain assessment.

Epictetus believed that circumstances shouldn't stop you from what you could be. You just need to have an accurate read and understanding of those circumstances and have an optimistic perspective. Let's take a look at this moment of Epictetus's life: His leg was broken due to torture. He couldn't change the fact of being a slave, and he didn't have the physical strength to stop his torturer. However, he decided to endure. He was lame, but he focused on his healthy leg and how he could still manage to walk. His ability to think and willingness to teach made him powerful. Those things could never be taken away by slavery or torture.

Adversity will eventually come. It is senseless to fuel fear or sorrow. Instead, persist and resist nurturing patience and tolerance.

A Roman Senator: Seneca

Lucius Seneca is an example of stoicism in many senses. First of all, he stood on the other extreme of the social scale, from Epictetus being contemporaries. He was a statesman and advisor to the young Roman Emperor Nero. He was powerful and rich. The same system of ideas was suitable for the slave and the statesman. However, Seneca's life is also an example of how power and wealth don't guarantee happiness, and are, instead, ephemeral and variable. His position close to power would ultimately seal his fate.

Even though he didn't pursue fame, his thoughts and lessons transcended centuries and still influence people's lives. He was an intellectual and a philosopher by profession. He became famous for his essays and letters to his friend Lucius, to whom he advised on friendship, moral obligations, humility, self-awareness, and self-improvement.

You might think that being a member of the government and having so much power gave Seneca a better life than Epictetus. It wasn't like that at all. His life was framed by the first five emperors of Rome's reigns, and it was a very violent period. There was a lot of social unrest, repression, and uncertainty. Surrounded by chaos, Seneca left some key teachings to remember. Here we share a summary of the most remarkable points (Daily Stoic, 2019).

There is nothing material and external worthy enough to take your inner calm

The only thing you can't get back if you waste it is time. You don't even realize how much time you dedicate to earn the things you later fear losing. How much time in your life do you have to dedicate to working just to buy stuff? Seneca thought about this many years ago, but is still a sign of our times.

Are you aware of the motivations for everything you do? Have you ever wondered if they are essential for you or if they just respond to social expectations, routine, or any other shallow reason? Are you doing it to please someone else?

Learn what you really want for yourself

It is mandatory to say *no* when you have to. Do you remember how Zeno learned from his first teachers that the most frequent problem is the irrepressible tendency to say *yes* almost immediately? If you think about it, you will find uncountable situations in your life when you said yes, and you ended up doing things you didn't want to, or later regret.

It is senseless to regret, and also to blame yourself. It is in the past and there is nothing you can change about it. What is past belongs to the externals. (You might notice how every concept is related and consistent with each other). This teaches that when you know what you want, there won't be a waste of energy and time on things that don't really matter.

Anger is a toxic emotion

Even when it can boost action, the consequences are never good because it isn't grounded in virtue. And if it doesn't go along with virtue, then it is against the natural order.

Seneca said that anger and rage are rooted in the wish of hurting others. The point here isn't to judge the right to be angry or react against injustice, for instance. It is about highlighting the potentially dangerous nature of anger. The wish to harm, to cause pain to others, takes our actions out of our control. How others will feel, and what type of reactions anger will trigger, are completely out of control.

Opposing ideas can open and improve your vision of life

Even when you know other people are wrong about their beliefs, there is always something you can learn. Opposing ideas aren't a threat to your convictions. Instead, being compelled to defend your position encourages you to review your rational arguments to support them.

Seneca also said that people live restrained by everything that frightens them, and frustrated, wishing for what they can't achieve. It makes people live in a rush to pursue more and more, feeling misfortune for what they lack instead of enjoying what they *do* have.

One of Seneca's most powerful statements says: "You are afraid of dying but how is the way that you are living any different from being dead" (Daily Stoic, 2019)? A familiar fashionable quote would be "live the life you choose to live." But what underlies your choice? Seneca advises: Make the most of this moment.

A Roman Emperor: Marcus Aurelius

Marcus Aurelius was born in 121, and he was the fifth of the so-called Good Emperors of Rome. He belonged to one of the wealthiest families in the Empire, and all his predecessors were patricians—the highest class in Roman society—dedicated to politics. From his early years, he lived the comfortable life of a patrician and prepared to perform his future role as a military strategist and a statesman (Biographics, 2020). Surrounded by luxury and power, Marcus Aurelius cultivated Stoic ideas based on his readings of Epictetus's writings and other Greek Stoic philosophers (Kamtekar, 2017).

He was probably the most powerful man on Earth at that time, but still, his life as an emperor wasn't easy at all. Having to face a devastating plague, a severe economic crisis and barbaric invasions, and severe health conditions, he trained himself to keep tight control of his emotions and fears, and amidst an empire enveloped in absolute chaos. The true fortitude and character of a person are shown not in times of peace, but in times of trouble. He is recalled as the Philosopher King.

His principal lessons have been retrieved from his own writings. His greatest work is *Meditations*, a book where he reflects on his vicissitudes as an emperor during the last years of the tough military campaigns he led against the Germans on the borders of the Roman Empire. Besides his *Meditations*, Marcus Aurelius' ideas have been conveyed from his official and personal correspondence, and other documents he wrote. The exchange of letters with his friends and teachers began before he was 20 and continued throughout his life (Kamtekar, 2017).

Marcus Aurelius somehow restored the teachings of all the previous Stoic philosophers, with a deep reflection on the ideas and practical application of each of their principles. Being an emperor, he constantly found himself wrapped in situations that tested his Stoic temper. In the *Meditations*, he makes a confession that might reflect how most of us feel in daily life: It is not possible to live as a philosopher. Marcus Aurelius appreciated a life dedicated to contemplation and reflection, but he was, and he was compelled to be, a man of action (Kamtekar, 2017). If you are wondering what you can have in common with a Roman emperor, you shall be surprised to know that along with the greatest troubles of one of the most powerful men in history, he also faced the little tribulations that torment any of us: How can I deal with someone who annoys me? What can I do to make an accurate decision in a complicated situation? How can I relieve distress and fear?

We can summarize his greatest contributions to stoicism not only as a philosophical school but as a practical way to improve our quality of life today, almost two thousand years later.

He believed that you should feel content with whatever happens, even if it isn't what you expected. He cultivated acceptance supported by the idea that there isn't any objective reality. Everything that surrounds you is a result of your opinions and perceptions. Therefore, reality is shaped by how you deem it. Marcus Aurelius didn't promote avoiding pain or struggles; Instead, he believed that even negative circumstances could lead to learning and gaining wisdom (Mr. Smart, 2020c).

It is possible to have a sense of contentment, no matter what happens, when you have embraced the commitment to search for virtue and understood the essence that underpins all human beings. Then, if someone hurt you or wished you ill will, you shouldn't feel anger. It's impossible to know what motivated other people to act against you, even if they told you. It is out of your control. All you can be sure about is that there are infinite perspectives, and that person that hurt you, has one of their own. That is what you must be aware of. Don't waste your energy being angry, better try to see things from the other's perspective and use it to be wiser.

Marcus Aurelius knew that anger was probably one of the major toxic emotions to deal with being a ruler. Nonetheless, he found in stoicism the means to control it. He didn't mean to repress emotions or deny the adversities happening around him, but as a Stoic, he believed life is the result of your opinions and there is always a way to approach reality from an optimistic angle (Mr. Smart, 2020c).

The other pillar of Marcus Aurelius' mindset was acceptance of what can't be changed or manipulated. He believed that there are two ways to deal with reality: The first is accepting things as they come; the second, adapting to the new scenario. There are inevitable events every person has to face: defeats, losses, pain, and so many others. There is a part of the indomitable nature of the cosmos that falls out of our control. Therefore, there is nothing we can do but accept them, and later, adapt to the new circumstances. Acceptance is perceived as an accommodation for what eventually occurs, and adapting is the ability to align your purposes to new conditions (Mr. Smart, 2020c).

As a man who had to face wars, betrayals, social unrest, political crisis, and defiance from his own allies, the ability to keep anger under control, and turn every hardship into an opportunity to become strengthened, was key to maintaining his power. He wrote in his *Meditations* that if obstacles are in the way, they are the way (Mr. Smart, 2020c). This brings back the idea of absolute acceptance of destiny guided by natural order. In simpler words, if you have to deal with it, you deal with it.

But keeping his throne safe, veiling for the reign, and integrity weren't Marcus Aurelius's only concerns. As a philosopher and as a Stoic, he thought that human nature is meant to search for virtue, and it implied conducting always justly. In his position as a statesman, it would have been easy for him to recur to any sort of means to achieve a goal. Instead, he strongly believed in the two aspects that distinguish humanity: rationality and sociality (Kamtekar, 2017). These two concepts provoked a reinforced commitment to justice and social welfare. He wrote in *Meditations* (Marcus Aurelius, 2006): "Just as you, yourself are a complementary part of a social system, so too your every action should complement a life of social principle. If any action of yours, then, does not have direct or indirect relation to the social end, it pulls your life apart and destroys its unity."

Reason enables us to understand and accept the course of fate, but also to decide the right direction to move on. That is, what is in line with virtue? On another hand, sociability is what links each of us to the rest of the community, since every individual is a meaningful part of the cosmos as a unity. If we pursue selfish goals deceiving those around us, we shall be thrown away from the path of virtue and further from *eudaimonia.*

Chapter 4:

Change Your Mindset - What Would A Stoic Do?

In the three previous chapters, you have read about what stoicism is and how it was first developed. We talked about four former Stoics that laid the foundations of this philosophical school. So far, you learned some about ancient philosophy and a bit of history, but you came to this book searching for clues to framing a way of life that alleviates trivial and not-so-trivial tragedies that badger you. We haven't put straight yet how the Stoic philosophy leaks from the academic molds to encompass your day-to-day activities.

Even if we assume philosophy as a way of life and not just as an intellectual approach is a nice statement, it is still about grabbing concepts and somehow engaging yourself in the pursuit of 'the truth.' Who has the time for that? Modernity drives people to move at such a hurrying pace that it is hard to conceal a philosophical attitude with the urgency of complying with duties and meeting objectives. Ancient Stoics seem to have found the cornerstone to feeling fulfilled and happy. However, how is that supposed to help you here, in the 21st century, with everything spinning around you at the speed of light?

Perhaps you have felt somewhat like Zeno when your business went to the wall, or you lost your job and had to start over from scratch. Epictetus or Seneca's stories might sound less familiar: Even though the routine somehow enslaves us, it is quite different from what Epictetus went through; and not many of us have to deal with a despot chief like Seneca did with Nero. We are not sure that even the CEO of a large international company would find themselves reflected on Marcus Aurelius' concerns with the Barbarians menacing the empire's boundaries. They experience different kinds of pressure.

However, it is not a coincidence that stoicism has become a powerful theoretical current in the last decades, and not only in academic environments. Modern life is making most of the Stoics' principles more relevant and necessary. Unluckily, this set of principles isn't a hat you can just put on and wear to live your life philosophically, following the cosmic order and flowing the stream. The world is far different from ancient times. Self-reflection and self-cultivation are insufficient to respond to all the externals that are right there, waiting for you at the traffic lights, in the meeting room, and every time you turn on the news. Wouldn't you like to see Zeno checking his reversals in the cryptocurrency market? How would Marcus Aurelius have reacted if he had to face a lockdown and have all of his earnings retained? Is it possible to just be carried along with the flow while you keep being rejected in your job interviews? What are the chances to resist and persist while the maturity of the mortgage is a part of that irrepressible flow?

Indeed, current life has a lot of hardships that ancient philosophers couldn't have even imagined. Today's world is characterized by constantly increasing uncertainty and limitless growing objectives. No matter how far you get, there is always something greater you need to go for. The sense of completeness and satisfaction is scarce and momentary. This all sounds awfully disheartening, doesn't it?

Pessimism and discouragement are your worst enemies. Life might feel overwhelming, but you have the resources to succeed in it. Besides, something hasn't changed from ancient times until now: We, people, wish to be happy. This chapter intends to find in former stoicism some guidelines to read our current time. Stoicism needs to be geared and some of its principles have missed relevance, but it endures due to its rational and spiritual essence as a philosophy of social engagement and love for humankind (Cleary, n.d.). To update the Stoic approach to current days, we shall try to imagine these Stoic remarkable figures in nowadays situations and picture how they would have reacted, or acted, to use the accurate Stoic term.

How to Think Like a Stoic

Now, you will read about some situations that tested the former Stoics' temperance, prudence, and indifference. Then, you will find a parallelism with familiar situations and verify how the Stoics' reactions would work to face them successfully.

Zeno's Last Coin

Let's go back to the day when Zeno's shipment sank into the Aegean sea. He found himself alone and with the last coin in his pocket. What would he do to move on with just a small budget? We don't know how Zeno felt in those first moments. Perhaps he felt being dragged into despair, worried, puzzled. He was just a merchant by then. His biographers tell us that, despite emotions, he pulled himself together and headed to a library in the Athenian *Agora*. With the little money he had left, he bought a copy of Xenophon's *Memorabilia of Socrates*. After reading it, he asked, probably the shopkeeper, where he could find a philosopher. Politics and philosophy were the frequent activities of Athenians, so the man must have told him that he would meet some of those at any public place. That is how Zeno ran into the Cynics, learned from them, and soon after, founded his own school (Sharpe & Blackford, 2017).

This was Zeno's reaction in front of this sudden change in his living conditions: He didn't struggle with what couldn't be modified. The goods were gone and they couldn't be recovered from the seabed. He couldn't buy a new ship and start over his merchant business. He couldn't get back at anybody for all his misery, since it was caused by nature. A storm that provoked his shipwreck. It made no sense to blame nature. He couldn't expect it to pay him back for the damage, could he?

So, what did he do? He had already heard about the Cynics and their teachings about accepting and living in line with nature. Therefore, Zeno used the last resources he had to turn the rudder around. If he couldn't recover his past life, he would invest in building a new one, with the resources he had left: a coin, and a new perspective. He drew a new plan for his life based on the actual conditions. He first had to understand, discarding everything that was out of reach, and then figure out what was that he could effectively do. The coin wouldn't buy him a new ship and goods, but it served to obtain a new vision. Zeno made an intelligent investment in his resources. Choose wisely how you will spend your last coin.

Epictetus in Front of Pain

Epictetus became lame after tough torture. The torturer punished him excessively and ended up breaking his leg. He was never able to recover from that injury. He was a slave, so he was at the complete mercy of his master. Today, we think of slavery to be unjust and against human dignity, but for ancient Romans, it was just another role in society. Slaves were aware of their condition and their absolute lack of rights. Only a few intended to rebel against the system. You might have heard of Spartacus and the rebellion he led and was fiercely repressed by the authorities.

We can't assure that Epictetus had learned a lesson from Spartacus's failed revolution, but his Stoic mindset taught him that the man who bought him as a slave could master his body but not his thoughts and emotions. Those still belonged to him. Think of the moment when Epictetus was being tortured. Pain is a physical reaction, and it is beyond our control. If your bones break, you can't stop the pain. That's nature. But you can choose how that pain will impact you.

Epictetus was able to withstand torture because he focused on what nobody could steal from him: His inner endurance. Stoics believed that the body, even being a part of the self, was beyond control, so physical pain was one of the externals to ignore. When Epictetus was being tortured, and his oppressor was twisting his leg, he didn't beg him to stop or try to escape. Instead, Epictetus warned him that it would break as it eventually did. While the other reactions placed the results in externals, Epictetus clung to patience and endurance, the things that he and not his oppressor could control. He could be patient and wait until the circumstances changed again, and he could endure resisting.

Epictetus became lame and the disability to walk accompanied him for the rest of his life. Did Epictetus feel pity for himself? Did he fuel resentment against his oppressor or his master? No, he decided to use it for his benefit:

> Sickness is an impediment to the body, but not to the will, unless itself pleases. Lameness is an impediment to the leg, but not to the will; and say this to yourself with regard to everything that happens. For you will find it to be an impediment to something else, but not truly to yourself (Daily Stoic, n.d.b, para 19).

Seneca's Worst Stroke of Luck

Ancient Roman society was deeply unequal. While patricians had full rights, plebs only had some of the political rights, even under the Republic. However, both groups had the privilege to be free and enjoy full civilian rights. Slaves, like Epictetus, were condemned to be treated as goods. Even after obtaining their freedom, slaves were never considered citizens of Rome. From this point of view, Seneca had been favored by fortune being born into a wealthy patrician family with close connections to power.

Seneca was raised in the city and received the education to perform as a statesman. He had a successful career as a Senator and had a strong influence on the emperors. This was good and bad luck at the same time. Seneca wasn't afraid to speak his mind out and that constantly got him in trouble. He was exposed to public scorn and his reputation was put under suspicion. Thus, he was even sent to exile in Corsica for years.

As a Stoic, Seneca had learned that there was no good or bad in things or people, just the inner attitude he could stand in front of each circumstance he had to face. Seneca could have chosen an easy life as a magistrate, but as the Stoic he was, he was concerned about the destiny of Rome. Therefore, Seneca tried constantly to step close to the rulers, searching for the opportunity to advise and seek the good of the state. Nonetheless, his interventions weren't always welcome.

Some of his biographers tell an interesting irony that once saved his life. On one occasion, he made a presentation in front of emperor Caligula, who was a despot. The emperor decided to put Seneca to death, but then he learned that the senator suffered from a terminal disease. There is no historical evidence to prove if that was true or a rumor, but Caligula believed it. Therefore, the emperor decided to let him live as he would eventually die within a short time, suffering before. The misfortune of his illness, or harmful rumor, saved Seneca's life. An example of how you shouldn't complain about your current conditions as they aren't intrinsically good or wrong. It is a matter of perspective and what you decide to do with them.

Later, Seneca's life wouldn't become any simpler as he turned to be Nero's tutor. We won't discuss Nero's controversial figure but we can say that he is remembered for his cruelty and tumultuous manner to rule. It must have been really difficult for Seneca to deal with such a pupil. Among the many atrocities ascribed to him, Nero accused Seneca of being part of a conspiracy to assassinate him, and this time, he was condemned to death (Bologna, 2021).

Marcus Aurelius and the Strength of Nature

When the time for Marcus Aurelius to become an emperor arrived, he was just a teenager. Although he was already prepared, being intellectually formed and with a complete *cursus honorum* (the political career), his rise to the imperial throne was postponed. The current emperor on his deathbed adopted another man, Antoninus Pius, to rule until Marcus Aurelius was older and more capable of ruling. The new heir to the crown committed to leaving the power as soon as Marcus Aurelius was ready. Despite his promise, Antoninus kept the throne for over two decades.

In ancient Rome, this would have provoked conspiracy and assassination of the man that could be accused of usurping the throne. Instead, Marcus Aurelius didn't do anything to reclaim his right to become the emperor. He prioritized his relationship with Antoninus and accepted his decision. He waited patiently until nature solved the issue for him.

After Antoninus's death, when it was finally the moment for Marcus Aurelius to assume, he found a new atypical circumstance that would prove his temper. He had an adopted brother with the same right as him to access the throne. While for any other heir, it would have unchained a civil war or a palace coup to get rid of the opponent, it didn't result in a conflict for a Stoic. Marcus didn't make any move against his brother. Instead, they both assumed power and ruled under a dual reign (Kings and Generals, 2020).

Although Marcus Aurelius had a deep sense of justice and was a highly skilled military strategist, his labor as an emperor wasn't easy. On one hand, he managed to keep the aristocracy satisfied and loyal to him, proving him to be a resourceful politician. On another hand, he had to defend the empire's boundaries from invaders in Asia Minor, and with that mission, he sent legions to successfully fight and push back the Parthians. Despite these triumphs that could be attributed to his traits as a ruler, Marcus Aurelius had to deal with two natural enemies that put his reign in danger: Torrential rain that flooded the Tiber River and later, a smallpox epidemic that the legionnaires brought from their campaign. Both events killed a significant part of the population with a direct impact on taxes collection (Kings and Generals, 2020). The strength of nature demonstrated to Marcus Aurelius that against it, his human power meant nothing.

How Do People React to Challenges Today?

In this section, we shall not try to make a direct analogy with the situations we have described. Probably, none of you have lost everything to a shipwreck, or are deprived of any of your rights due to social categorization. You aren't either the counselor of a despot king, and conspiracy accusations aren't hanging over your head. And finally, it is unlikely that you are an emperor fighting enemies' armies and plagues at the same time. Still, these lines about these Stoics' lives show us how being and acting as a Stoic is never easy but always the best option. If you think about each of the stories again, you might notice that what they did, were, in fact, reasoned choices. Any other response would have led them to greater tragedies.

Now, let's try to reflect on some typical situations in our modern life and see what these Stoic responses provided by Zeno, Epictetus, Seneca, and Marcus Aurelius can teach you to move into the world.

Zeno's Initiative

How many times did you have to start over in your life? You can think of the first time you started job research, and you had to prepare your resume, deal with the lack of experience, and have one interview after another, and it seemed like your profile would never meet the employer's expectations. Perhaps, Zeno reminded you of the time you invested all your savings in a new business and it didn't work out. The sense of having your hands empty again.

Sometimes, it isn't about what you lose but what you have to drop. For example, it might have happened that you had the best job you could strive for and then you realize it just doesn't match your personal goals anymore. The career you chose, the city where you live, the workplace you have to attend to every day… They just don't make you happy.

Sometimes, you feel like you are bottoming out for other non-economic variables. Getting a divorce or needing to decide it, or breaking up with close relationships—couples, friends, partners, family—are also losses that seem to take you back to square one.

You have surely been through at least one of those situations. Perhaps you are currently going through some of them. How would you describe your reactions? Are you feeling disappointed? We share the common belief that life is always about moving upwards. If you have to stop, stir to the sides, or even go back, it is branded as a failure. What a terrible word! It is paralyzing when you think you have failed. It is almost impossible to get any good from that sense. Failure comes along with the worst emotions.

Do you think Zeno felt he failed when he became dispossessed? Perhaps it was easier not to blame himself because it was the wildness of nature that caused his shipwreck, but still, he could have handled the ship better, made more assertive decisions to avoid the storm, or been more cautious with his business. Whereas, Zeno didn't spend time in remorse. Instead, he accepted his new circumstances and made decisions adopting a new perspective. He had a few coins in his pocket and he thought about what he could actually do with them. Where could those resources take him? How could his life be from then on? Those are interesting questions to replace guilt and a sense of failure. Make it simple: What are you going to do with the coins left in your pockets? There is always something left by the storm.

Epictetus's Endurance

Through Epictetus's life and the event that left him lame, you can find a strong example to reflect on how you deal with health issues. As ancient Stoics said, your body doesn't belong to the realm of what is under your control. You can and must take care of your physical and mental health, but illnesses and accidents eventually happen to you, and to your loved ones. Is it possible to accept pain and suffering with such patience and resignation for ordinary people? Was Epictetus one of a kind? Epictetus's endurance in front of torture and his destiny don't seem meant for any typical person.

Science and medicine evolve to find the cure for all types of illnesses and make progress in discovering treatments and vaccines. However, we continue to hear about new diseases or even the comeback of some that were even extinguished. People now have more access to information to take care of their health, but at the same time, the routine and the increasing burdens from our style of life hamper our options. We sleep and eat as we can, live constantly in a rush, and have very little time to exercise and be in contact with nature. Along with increased comfort, more hazards seem to surround us. What would Epictetus do in our shoes?

The slave Stoic tells you that your pain and illness don't define you. Rather than that, it is you who decides what to do with them. If you or someone in your family have recently received a severe diagnosis, or if you are already under any painful treatment, you will probably think that you aren't Epictetus. You, like any of us, aren't prepared to suffer. Perhaps that is a lesson to learn from this Stoic: You need to prepare yourself to suffer.

When an expected or premature loss happens, or if you have to struggle with long-term diseases, you might wonder: *Why me? Why is life so cruel to me? What could you have done wrong to deserve such a punishment?* It is a very human reaction. But, on another hand, if you simply turn around, you will notice that everybody has their own tragedies, and suffering is written in human nature as well as the search for happiness. If you could relieve your pain just by being aware that it happens to everybody all the time, it would be too easy. And that isn't what stoicism teaches. It is not easy. However, it is simple.

Epictetus teaches you that endurance in front of pain comes from inner strength, and not from others' suffering. You need to give pain or illnesses the appropriate space in your life: They are just a part of the conditions. Instead of considering a limitation, try to objectively think of what you can do in spite of your pain. Own it. Rule it. Will it still hurt? Probably, but at least you will still be on your path to search for virtue and live a fulfilling life.

Seneca and the Risks You Want to Run, or Not

Through Seneca's life, you had the opportunity to see how privileges can become a disadvantage. Despite his accommodating status within Roman society, power and his closeness to the emperors became his nightmare. Nonetheless, Seneca wouldn't complain to fate about these conditions. He could have chosen a relaxed political life like many other senators, just getting involved in the inevitable matters. Instead, he chose to step into the public arena to influence the rulers and to fight for the common good. As a Stoic, he believed in the coincidence between collective and individual purpose in life. Every person has to decide more than once in life if they are going to commit or be slipshod. Seneca made his choices. What do you think he would advise you?

There are two possible situations you might be in. Let's assume you have a management position with some relative power. While for some people this can be a synonym for success, it can also be absolutely overwhelming: You have to constantly make decisions that impact you and other people, and you make yourself accountable for what you do and others do, which technically falls out of your control but still is part of your duties, and then, you have to fix what went wrong. Is that what you want for your life? Are those roles aligned with your personal goals? Are you sure that everything you do is contributing to the collective goal? You are not compelled to take that responsibility, but you have to make the choice. If you don't want to deal with all that, then you should think if that is the role you decide to play.

On the other hand, you can be at the other end of the rope. Most people don't have management jobs. You would rather be in an employee position, with several rules to follow without objection, deadlines you didn't schedule to meet, and partners you didn't choose to work with. What do you have in common with Seneca at this point? Everything. You are still accountable for every decision you make, and even though you wouldn't notice it, anything you do—or don't—impacts others. Remember what Stoics thought about the natural order: Everything has a specific place and role, tightly linked to the whole. If you cut a thread of a piece of clothing, what do you think will happen?

In this situation, you might feel your role is irrelevant, or it won't guide you to accomplish your goals. Are you considering your job, your present activities, and your current relationships separated from what you believe is your purpose in life? Then, what are you waiting for to start acting? Whining and nurturing frustration is pointless. That won't take you any closer to your goals. The Stoics would say that no one but yourself will take responsibility for where you are or what you do. So, you shouldn't be wasting time blaming circumstances or cursing your bad luck. It isn't about becoming a senator or fighting for a management position. It is about taking action to be where you decide to be. What do you think Seneca would have done if he was a simple plebeian in charge of his farm instead of a patrician? Don't you think he would have tried to be the best farmer?

Wait for It and Take Your Opportunity

Marcus Aurelius's life brings us a lesson of greatness. He knew he was the legitimate heir to the throne and, although he could have done things to precipitate the events, he decided to wait. He just let it be self-evident. He teaches us that good things take time, and you must be well prepared. Marcus Aurelius is an example of civic responsibility as he assumed power to work for the common good, the integrity, and the peace of the empire he ruled. He had a clear notion of what power and influence on people can do. Personal and collective purposes were perfectly aligned.

In the latter sense, Marcus Aurelius behaved similarly to Seneca. They dedicated their lives to growing virtue. The Roman Emperor also encourages you to assume commitment and responsibility, whatever your role in society might be. Moreover, it is also interesting to analyze how Marcus Aurelius reacted to all the obstacles he found until he achieved the greatest goal.

How many times have you thought about asking for a promotion? You deserve it; you have worked hard and are skilled enough. Out of nowhere, you see that someone else gets it before you do. That person is usurping your place. Let's see another example. Sometimes when you study for hours to pass an exam, but you are asked questions you don't remember, or you get so nervous that you draw a blank. Other students who studied much less than you just receive the easy questionnaire or are lucky enough to guess the correct answers. How unfair is that?

The right question is: Does it matter? What is your real purpose? To be good at your job and make the best of it, learn and develop your skills, or just compare your achievements to others? Do you intend to prove to anybody but yourself what you are capable of doing? Who are you competing with? If you measure your goals with others' standards, you will always feel dissatisfied with extra pressure on your shoulders, just because there are a lot of people with similar objectives and talents, and who are even higher skilled than you.

Whenever you feel discouraged, remember Marcus Aurelius: The throne of the Roman empire, the most coveted and powerful position in his times, was meant for him. And his tutor, and his brother, and plagues and floods stood in his way. He waited patiently for his opportunity, and when it came, he did his best.

Stoicism as the Standard Way of Behavior

Stoicism has indeed proved to be an effective way of life for people of all social statuses, from slaves to emperors, in ancient times and the 21st century. However, it shouldn't be rendered in a general assumption that every person would react in the same way in similar circumstances. Stoicism has a base of common rules to understand and be in the world, but it isn't the denial of particular interests. Individuality and singularity of every human being are, in fact, a part of that basis of principles.

In a nutshell, this means that you must follow the stories and examples as a guideline to reflect on your own life. Nonetheless, your decisions and reasoned choices can only be determined by your own experience. Remember that stoicism is rooted in the conviction of living in perfect harmony with nature, and nobody but you can know better the spot of nature where you're standing right now.

If you continue to read and make it this far, the first stage is complete: You are determined to pursue happiness through virtue. The next steps are simple (Not easy!). You are about to start a two-way journey: One, directly into your inner self, to unveil who you are, and which is your purpose. The other part of the trip is to the outside, the environment, your reality. There, you will find your starting point and the last coins in your pocket, just like Zeno did.

Chapter 5:

How To Use Stoicism To Improve Your Life

Now that we have taken a thorough look at the stoicism principal concepts, and seen how they reflected on the first Stoics' lives, we can delve into learning how to develop a Stoic mindset ourselves. Even though stoicism is a philosophical school, and as we have pointed out, concepts are relevant to understand the perspective to face reality, it is more of a practical way of life that can be achieved by cultivating the appropriate habits. There are no secrets. You just need to make the decision to discover the Stoic that dwells within you.

A Proper Mindset is the Foundation of Stoicism

Olympic athletes unable to display their best performances in the most cherished tournament are more common than we would expect. Why does this happen? No athlete goes to the Olympic games without the appropriate training. They all go through high-yield competitions and are considered elite sportsmen and women. Even so, we have seen many of these remarkable athletes being prematurely disqualified in the early stages, falling short of their own marks, and even giving up before starting. Some of them have said that all they could think about was that they wanted the competition to be over (Cohn, n.d.). Even when they need a winning mentality, it is clear that no matter how professional and experienced they are, it is not enough to perform at their best. The secret reason why Olympic athletes are able to perform at such a high level isn't hidden in the physical preparation. The real challenge is battling the mind.

It sounds like a *cliché*, but it doesn't make it less true. The exceptional source of strength is our mind. In the case of athletes, some coaches work on stilling a particular mindset: The *Just happy to be here* mentality. Does it ring a bell? This mentality promotes the ability to focus on the moment, enjoy the process, and feel the experience instead of putting all the expectations on the results. There are many competitors and only three will get to the podium. They certainly need something more.

The analogy with sports isn't eventful. Ancient Greeks found a direct and tight relationship between the mind and the body. It was over two thousand years before science was able to explain how the mind and the brain aren't different things, but instead, work together. The brain and its physiological functions influence and determine our emotions. In the opposite direction, our emotions can alter our perception of reality and our decisions. Here's the reason why the mind and body need to be in perfect equilibrium.

For Stoics, the attitude of indifference toward anything that couldn't be controlled by our willingness didn't mean the carelessness of the body. It is out of our control as long as we can still get hurt or catch a disease, but it doesn't mean that you aren't accountable for it. Seneca famously said in one of his letters: "Be rigorous with the body, that it may not be disobedient to the mind" (Loeb & Henderson, n.d.). This statement refers to the good habits you must grab to educate your body so it won't be weaker than your mind. In the same letter, he explained how you should attend to your physical needs just to keep in good health. It sounds obvious, but it is not. How often do you have frugal meals because you are in a hurry? When you aren't hungry, how often do you eat as much as you can? How much time do you dedicate to sleep and training? If you don't train your body as a Stoic, then you can't expect it to respond to your mind.

Marcus Aurelius was a weak and sickly child, and everybody believed that he would never be strong enough to play a solid role as an emperor. In ancient times, politics was more than rhetoric. The emperor was expected to lead military campaigns, which implied strong and healthy bodies. Therefore, Marcus Aurelius was looked upon with reserve. The emperor agreed with Seneca and also wrote that "a healthy mind could only exist with a healthy body" (Vargas, 2022, para 7), although overload exercise could lead to vanity. The compass is always a virtue.

The emperor had drawn himself a routine to train and educate his body to serve his mind. He went running every morning before starting his duties. Nature calls on everything to move in the universe. Why would human beings be the exception? Marcus Aurelius understood that to be in harmony with the cosmos, he had to accompany that natural impulse to be in constant movement. Besides, he had learned that sometimes running or walking was an excellent method to clear his mind.

Developing Skills to Affront Difficulties

One of the four pillar virtues of stoicism is courage. Life isn't easy. Sometimes it isn't simple either. But Stoics are convinced of the gift it is and the importance of enjoying it, of embracing it regardless of all the adversities to come. Stoicism prompts you to be courageous in a physical way. First, by knowing your body and taking care of it, and standing when something happens, committing in soul and body to face the odds. But there is even more than that. Being courageous also demands making the best choices and doing the right thing.

We have already explained how virtue is found in the golden mean: You don't need to wear a superhero coat and roam the streets fighting crime to prove your courage and reinforce your stoicism. Courage goes hand in hand with wisdom. You will need to implement Zeno's maxim to separate between the "preferred and dispreferred indifferents' (Hanselman, n.d.). Like everything, it is all a matter of habits. You can develop the required skills to recognize what your battles are. You learn to choose which of them to fight, and which you can let go of.

In Chapter 4, we had a lot of examples of how each of the former fathers of stoicism had diverse living conditions that could have determined their destiny. Instead of giving in, they persisted and found a way to use them as leverage to display the best version of themselves. Epictetus teaches us a valuable lesson about how to make it possible. He used the word *integrity* to define how you should place yourself in the roles you have to play, and do it the best you can. Epictetus said that you are the one who best knows yourself (Pigliucci, 2018). So, no one but you knows what to expect.

What do you have to do to display your best version? In the first place, you must identify your personal weaknesses and strengths. And here we shall underline *personal.* It is important not to confuse the socially shaped stereotypes for what is considered weak or strong. Let's share a very illuminating example: We started the section talking about sports. Different sports require different types of bodies: basketball and volleyball need people with a height over the average, sprinters are faster than the rest, wrestlers are physically stronger, and so on. It would be a huge mistake to consider that basketball players are weak sportsmen or women because they aren't good sprinters, right? Well, that is the way to establish the parameters to recognize what your weaknesses are.

You might notice how every new idea perfectly fits in the Stoic whole system. Your weaknesses and strengths aren't determined by others' judgments or any other type of external. If an external hampers your ability to thrive, remember Epictetus and his lame leg. He realized that his inability to walk like the rest wasn't really a weakness. He decided that it wouldn't be. So, first, you must take a thorough look inwardly and discern which your personal weaknesses are but not compared to others or illusionary interpretations of reality. Try to figure out which of your personal traits can block the way to achieving your purpose. If you are afraid of heights, it doesn't make you weak unless you have settled that your purpose is to be a commercial pilot or an astronaut.

Nonetheless, this is just the first step. Even though stoicism invites you to flow with the stream and cultivate steadiness, it won't lead to a passive attitude. That would be conformity and it tears you apart from the path of wisdom. You must remember Marcus Aurelius's words: The impediment to action advances action (Daily Stoic, n.d.b). You will notice how some of the Stoic fathers' words are brought over and over because they can be read in many different ways, depending on the context. Marcus Aurelius meant that whatever comes up in your way, you don't stop or go back: You figure out how to continue despite the obstacle.

In other words, you can try to revert your weaknesses. Small people can play basketball or volleyball, improve their technique, and become good players. Or you can drive all your energy into reinforcing your strengths. Don't blame genetics for not being taller. Don't give up sports because you can't be the ultimate champion. Learn what you can do and work to thrive.

Two amazing results will come out of this. First of all, you will accomplish the greatest goal, which is assuming your spot in the universe, doing your part, and cooperating with the collective realization of human perfection. But apart from this, you will learn to cherish yourself, and as Epictetus also said, you won't sell yourself cheap. Current societies constantly drive to put a price on yourself, and it isn't just metaphorically. How much do you earn for your knowledge, your expertise, and your lifetime? By knowing yourself, you will have a clear idea of when to say enough is enough. Remember Epictetus's words: "You are the one that knows yourself, of how much you are worth to yourself and for how much you are selling yourself... Consider at what price you sell your integrity: But please, for God's sake, don't sell it cheap." That is all you have got (Pigliucci, 2018).

Practical Applications Are a Byproduct of a Well-established Mindset

In the previous paragraphs, we discussed how the idea of weakness and strength shouldn't be measured with a general pattern. Stoicism assesses that there is a universal intelligible reason, but each individual is placed at a singular position within the cosmos and develops particular perceptions of their environment. It doesn't mean that there will be as many realities as individuals, but stoicism believes that it is more coherent with the search for collective and particular virtue when people focus on what they have in easy reach. The universe will continue to exist even if you can't explain it. But you need to read the coordinates of your life to learn your conditions and make reasoned choices.

A well-established mindset isn't a unique universal formula you can discover, memorize, and automatically apply randomly. Stoicism provides you with the guidelines to design your own roadmap. If you lack this, how will you know you are moving in the right direction? Stoicism principles are a sort of lighthouse to take you to safe harbor: If your steps are taking you toward virtue, then you continue confidently your way.

The mindset you need to settle for yourself must include:

- The instruments to interpret your current conditions.
- The purpose or goals you want to achieve aligned with the collective purpose of virtue.
- The awareness of the weaknesses that won't block you.
- The awareness of strengths that will make you persist, resist and thrive.

This mindset isn't just an abstract system of ideas. It must be rendered into specific actions in your routine. And, it can't be effectively developed without nurturing healthy habits to take care of your body. Like many other ancient Greek philosophical schools, Stoics gave the body a central importance. Your body is what actually places you in this world, the source of all your strengths, and enables you to pass from theory to action. Therefore, training your body is as relevant as creating your mindset. As Seneca said, your body needs to be educated to follow and obey your mind.

One of the biggest challenges Stoics face is dealing with emotions. They said that you shouldn't be a prisoner of passions as they trigger irrational emotions. Some of those passions are satisfied or not through your body. If you win the battle to control your physical appetites, you have one more step taken in the right direction.

On the other hand, your relationship with your body implies revisiting reality. Your body is the first and more approachable consciousness of the boundaries between you and the environment. This awareness provides a more accurate perception of where you stand and how your surroundings are. This increases assertive and effective judgment of how to live ethically and happily.

You might be wondering how you can appropriate this mindset and establish it to rule your life. What is the procedure for taking the ideas expressed in a book into real day-to-day activities? It isn't something you read and study, like scientific theories and formulas. You can't just repeat the words and provide correct answers. However, by learning the principles, you start seeing everything differently. In the following chapters, we will share practical exercises to transform these ideas into behaviors. Turn words into action.

The only way to live your life as a Stoic is to take each moment as a Stoic would do. If you think you don't have time to think, to make a pause before reacting, try to visualize the hours you probably spend overthinking about those issues that trouble you. When you can't fall asleep, being worried about your deadlines the next day. As you move into the Stoic mindset, you will learn to administer your time and energy to developing it. The key is to practice, think, and practice again.

Chapter 6:

Facing Challenges

How do you feel about challenges? We can assume that there are two types of people: Those who enjoy having some thrill in their life to cut the routine and keep moving. Some others just prefer to move smoothly through the events, enjoying the peace and being comfortable with stillness. Of course, stoicism has a word for both types: Steadiness and calm are necessary conditions to find virtue, and at the same time, life is about contending with the unexpected and changeable.

The Merriam-Webster dictionary (2023) provides different meanings for the term *challenge*. Let's focus on two. The first one in the list: Challenge is "a stimulating task or problem," but also "a summons that is often threatening, provocative, stimulating, or inciting." Challenges shouldn't be considered either what someone searches to experience enthusiasm or what shakes your life and makes you feel helpless and unstable. No matter if you go for them or evade them, challenges are a part of the uncontainable stream of life. The lesson to learn is how to flow with the stream while relishing stillness and not falling into despair when you have to stand up and be courageous.

How to Identify Your Current Challenges

When you tried to find yourself in the two types of challenging people described in the previous section, you might have thought that both are extreme. Most people appreciate some challenges to test their abilities and find extra motivation to improve. As the dictionary points out, it is something that stimulates. However, jumping from one challenge to another turns out to be exhausting, and many times, frustrating. Daily life already piles challenges on you that you didn't even ask for. You might find yourself thinking, for instance, *That's fine, I don't want to prove myself better any longer. I like it this way.*

Excessive challenges—we shall see if they are all real and unavoidable—put too much pressure on you and increase the levels of stress. This is a feeling perceived with a very negative connotation. It is usually assumed as "a feeling of emotional or physical tension. It can come from any event or thought that makes you feel frustrated, angry, or nervous" (MedlinePlus, 2022, para 1-2). If this becomes the customary sense in your life every day, it can make you feel overwhelmed, provoke mental and physical illnesses, and of course, be unhappy. The good news is that stress isn't *per se* a negative feeling. In fact, it is one of the natural resources human beings have to keep themselves alive, and with the appropriate mindset, you can learn to regulate it and use it to enhance your strengths.

The World Health Organization (WHO; 2023) defines stress as

> a state of worry or mental tension caused by a difficult situation. Stress is a natural human response that prompts us to address challenges and threats in our lives. Everyone experiences stress to some degree. The way we respond to stress, however, makes a big difference to our overall well-being.

You have surely heard everywhere that stress is harmful to your health and how important it is to reduce its levels and lower the risks of severe health emergencies. Some studies have delved into this matter to figure out how something produced by nature (a natural response) can be risky for health. One of these studies interviewed several people, and the results showed that many of them felt they had too much stress in their lives, but only a few feared it could be positively dangerous for them. Statistics taken from this study proved that stress became a factor of risk only for those who believed so (Gonigal, 2013). Here, you can perfectly see the power of your mind.

Mental health professionals have taught for years that stress is something to eliminate or reduce to the minimum, but that paradigm is changing. Instead, stress is considered a motivation to thrive, as the WHO's definition highlights.

You must notice that there are physical responses beyond your control when you are under pressure and feeling stressed: Your heart is beating faster, you sweat more than normal, and your breathing rhythm is altered. How can it be good to feel so bad? It isn't weird that for so long, and still for many physicians, these symptoms are still considered harmful. Whenever these symptoms appear, you tell yourself *'This is it, I'm dying... I'm having a heart attack.'* These episodes have been defined as anxiety crises.

The obvious question that emerges is how you can control those innate reactions. Remember what Seneca told us about the body: Be rigorous with the body, so that it may not be disobedient to the mind. You can subdue your body's reactions to your mind's commands. The adoption of a new mindset about stress will help you eliminate fear, so when these physical reactions come up, you will be totally aware that they are simply the manifestation of you being pushed forward.

A social stress test conducted by scholars showed that it is possible to have a positive perception of these physical changes when you are in a stressful situation: The increase in the cardiac beating means that you are being energized and getting prepared to face a challenge; The changes in the breathing are needed to drain more oxygen to the brain, so you are more alert and reactive. What surprised me the most about these results was that blood vessels didn't constrain if you focus on the idea that stress is the way your body responds when circumstances demand a bit more than normal from you. When you learn to see stress as a resource to improve, your body responds healthily despite the visible symptoms that might impress you for the bad (Gonigal, 2013).

Do you want to learn something more about this new friend? Stress is one of the brain's functions that makes us live in society. In a nutshell, stress is the physical response that makes human beings establish close bonds, care for each other, express feelings, and ask for help when they are in need (Gonigal, 2013). Can you see nature's wisdom?

Examples of Types of Challenges

Stoics believed that people assume different roles within societies, with a set of associated duties and relationships (Pigliucci, 2018). However, not every person performs each role in the same way, and the same person can behave differently depending on the roles' demands. Let's see this through some examples.

Parents

Among the infinite list we could name of challenges parents face constantly—and wishing there was a bigger word for it—we can assume that the worst of all we can think of is dealing with a child's illness. The sense of impotence for not being able to take your child's body and feel their pain instead. The anguish of waiting for the diagnosis, results, improvement, and alleviation. What are the proper words to describe what parents should do when they have to pass through a situation like this? What does stoicism have to tell them when it absolutely doesn't go with nature?

The first reaction parents experience when they receive a severe diagnosis for their children is to wonder or ask God, the universe, or whatever they believe in *Why me?* And the answer is very simple: *Why not?* This is probably the most complicated situation in life to behave like a Stoic. Emotions are very difficult to be repressed and there seem to be no reasoned choices for them. Nonetheless, they are: Whether you can run away from the pain, withdraw in yourself, or even surrender to suffering, or you can courageously assume the first duty as a parent which is to take care of your child. What do you think would be wiser and fairer than that?

Leaders

When we talk about leaders, we refer to all those who have a management position; it can be a formal role or not. You might be a CEO of a big company, an employer, or a business owner, but also you might be in charge of teams in civil organizations or sports associations. They all have leadership as a common denominator. Although leadership is usually related to having power and giving directions, it is much more than that. Leadership is defined as the ability to impact others' lives. Therefore, leaders are responsible for guiding the team and each of the collaborators to achieve a common goal. It represents a burden of responsibility to watch for everybody's well-being.

The challenges faced by leaders are diverse. It is not an easy task to understand and conciliate different positions. It doesn't matter if it is a work team or the church choir, the members can have particular objectives that don't perfectly match with the rest. Perhaps it is about the levels of satisfaction they perceive, the roles distributions, or just different purposes. It is a challenge for the leader to cope with singularities and identify in each of the team members who is the best for the group.

It is a challenge to interview candidates for a role and decide who gets the job and who continues to be unemployed. It is hard to decide on firing someone or assigning a promotion. And the list could continue. However, there is a great challenge all leaders deal with: change and the subsequent crisis that it usually brings. How do leaders cope with uncertainty? How do they accept the obstacles on the way and continue in spite of them?

Entrepreneurs

This is probably one of the most challenging roles in a competitive, demanding environment. Even though you can embrace change as the pattern and not the exception, dealing with uncertainty is always a threatening challenge, especially to those that only have themselves. Entrepreneurs—and here we shall generalize—have to develop their activities with a tighter budget, and with a lot of competition, mostly from bigger companies. While not having a chief can be taken as an advantage, it puts a huge challenge to manage time effectively and keep a balance between knowing the limitations and being ambitious enough to not stagnate.

It isn't an easy matter to make all the decisions on your own, and be wise enough to identify when you have an opportunity to take in front of you, and when it can lead you to the abyss. If you are an entrepreneur, you take full accountability for your decisions, and they don't just matter in economic terms. Your entrepreneurship is more than a business: It is your life project. Every decision you make puts everything on the line.

Helpers

When referring to helpers, we think of all those people who don't occupy management roles and are in working relationships. You could be an employee, a caregiver in different types of institutions and organizations, or a shop assistant. Your role is defined by what you do to assist others in accomplishing their objectives. But does it mean that you don't have objectives of your own?

It is mistakenly believed that helpers can accomplish their assessments with lower levels of pressure and stress. They are only responsible for the activities they are assigned to do, but since they are just gear parts, the system continues to exist if they fail, or if they are replaced. Contrary to these ideas, helpers face constant daily challenges, as everybody else. If you are a helper, then you already know you have a double job to interpret what is expected from you and then execute it. There is a latent tension between doing what you must do, and what you would really want to do. Sometimes, the helping role does not match the personal purpose. Let's admit that there are too many roles in society that aren't anybody's dream, and yet society needs helpers to do it. It is a true challenge, and a tough one, to understand the major importance of everybody's role. It is a challenge to give credit for what you do, but also to leave that spot if it isn't fulfilling enough.

Why Are You "Not Capable?" Stop Struggling to Deal With This Challenge

The list of possible challenges you might be facing could be infinite, especially considering that you play more than one role in society. You are a father, a son, a chief, a partner, a citizen, and so on. It sounds a bit overwhelming, but this is the way life goes for everybody. The difference is that you have made the decision to reflect on the processes of dealing with challenges and recognize what prevents you from being as happy as you should be.

Some frequent challenges in very general terms:

- You don't like your job and you want to quit.
- Your boss is excessively demanding.
- You want to request a promotion, a salary increment, or a new role.
- You are being subjected to mistreatment by your superiors, workmates, colleagues, and members of your family.
- You want a change in your relationships: couples, siblings, parents, friends, and workmates.
- You don't like your job or your career.

Since this book intends to be a toolkit more than a theoretical compilation, you can continue to write your own list. We suggest behaving like a Stoic and, before dealing with them or going overthinking as you tend to do, try to implement Zeno's preferred and dispreferred indifference: Do you really have to cope with all those? Surely you can shorten the list a bit. Follow the Stoic principles to use that resource effectively: Wisdom and a sense of justice to discharge those that are irrelevant. Temperance and courage to go for the others.

What Turns That Issue Into a Challenge?

This question settles a difference between regular situations you can decide upon and continue and others that are perceived like a stone in the shoe. Sometimes, it is difficult to understand the reasons. You have taken thousands of decisions in your life, some of them more complex than others. You have applied to jobs, rejected and been rejected, failed and tried again, why is this matter so more complicated than the rest?

We want to share with you a simple exercise that will help you figure out what is different about this matter that worries you. The first step is to name it. You might know the feeling of being happy or sad, but can't really tell why. Sometimes, emotions don't need a lot of explanation, unless they become permanent. But here, we have another point. Sometimes, you postpone decisions or deny problems unconsciously. You internally know that something is waiting for you to act—we won't say *react*—but your mind tricks you and you aren't able to visualize what it is. The answer to that is fear. Can a Stoic be afraid of something? Fear, in fact, comes with human nature, so you don't struggle to avoid it. You learn to cope with it.

Tim Ferriss suggests a daily and rather simple exercise to name challenges and face the paralyzing fear that prevents you from acting. He invites you to observe first what the costs and advantages of action (what you should do about the issue) are, but apart from that, pay special attention to the potential costs of inaction (Ferriss, 2018). What can happen if nothing changes, if you just sit and stay still? Remember that the Stoic maxim of flowing with the stream isn't an invitation to inaction. Instead, it is about making the best decision to act.

Chapter 7:

Step 1—Stoic Approach to Dealing With Stress

Our starting point for this chapter is the full conception of stress as we defined it previously. Now you know that stress will not kill you, but you still must develop skills to handle healthy levels of stress. We can mention three steps to dealing better with stress:

- Step 1: Explore your routine and identify what circumstances and people put pressure on you.
- Step 2: Apply the preferred and dispreferred indifference: Choose your battles. You don't need to deal with everything.
- Step 3: Develop the Stoic mindset and make stress your friend.

Now, let's explore some aspects of your life that are the pillars of handling stress.

Health—The Body Is the Temple of the Mind

We discussed in Chapter 4 the importance of recognizing your body as the material vessel of who you are. It also represents the limits between you and the rest of nature. Seneca said once that the body carries your mind, and therefore you must dedicate time to keep it in shape: Train the body to submit to the mind so it won't rebel against the mind. Taking care of your body is a central issue for a Stoic way of life, and it implies watching your health since without it, you can't do much.

We shall take for granted some good habits that aren't exclusive to a Stoic mindset: Regular medical checks-up, avoiding the use of toxic substances, good rest and enough—though not excessive—sleeping hours, exercise, and a well-balanced diet. Those are basic recommendations that any self-conscious person would follow. But there is something different if we consider them from a Stoic approach.

Keeping a well-balanced diet and dedicating sufficient but not excessive time to rest are ways to train and educate your body to respond to vital necessities. Eating or sleeping needs to be administered reasonably to prevent them from turning into insatiable appetites. Remember that as Stoics taught, you mustn't let your body control your mind. You decide what and how much you eat, and how many hours you need to sleep. It is a way to mold your body in correspondence with your mind. If you can eat vegetables, why would you give your body harmful options like fatty food or sugars? If you know your body needs rest, why would you stay up late, either working or hanging around? Those aren't reasoned choices.

Exercise deserves some special words since it isn't only important to improve your metabolism but also helps you clear your mind. The German philosopher Nietzsche, at the beginning of the 20th century, talked about the benefits of really long walks, and by real walks, he meant six hours. You might be thinking *Who has the time to go for a six-hour walk?* Remember Marcus Aurelius. Can't you think of any busier man than a Roman Emperor with invaders and plagues all over the place? And still, he made it a routine to go running every morning. We don't know if he ran for six hours, but the point is that he found that moment a priority to keep his body strong and to help his mental focus.

Stoics gave physical training a lot of importance, not because they searched for the social standards of beauty, but because they considered it a contest. The weaknesses of the flesh shall be dominated by thoughtful minds. Stoics didn't recommend overloading your body or trying to grow your muscles because that isn't what will make you stronger. Seneca said that no matter how strong and big you get, nature is full of stronger animals than human beings (Benjamin, Personal power, 2020). But they did believe that exercise makes your body more proficient in responding better. For example, it helps you broaden your shoulders and your chest, and develops your lungs. That improves your breathing, and you are more likely to remain calm in disturbing situations (Daily Stoic, n.d.c).

Money: What Is Its Place in Your Life?

It would be unrealistic to propose a life without money, and stoicism always promotes being realistic. So, let's assume that money is our main means to obtain everything we need to survive. It is just something that we can't get rid of. Stoicism doesn't put forward the idea of leaving your job and your house and living from what nature provides. Nonetheless, it does compel you to settle a new conception about money and rethink the place you give it in your life. Instead of considering money for what it can buy, try to focus on the time you need to spend working to earn it. Then, ponder the impact of not having so many things. How much of your time are you willing to give up to get them?

It is a catchphrase that money doesn't buy happiness, but still, most people have money as one of their goals in life. That's not a part of the Stoic mindset because money just allows you to obtain things, and things aren't internal. Happiness comes with virtue, which can't be bought. You must learn to see money as the means, never the end.

When it comes to money, there are different types of people. Some take high risks and spend over what they can afford or invest everything they have to obtain higher gains. Others are more conservative and prefer saving for rainy days. And there is this other group with the basic idea that money is meant to be spent. Which type of person are you? This is not about being judgmental about who you are. We couldn't say that it is better to spend your money as there was no tomorrow, or save for a future you don't know depriving yourself of what you desire at the present. The secret is to learn what is your relationship with money and ground it on a reasonable basis.

Money and what to do with it is a common source of challenges, but the Stoic mindset allows more control over the impulse of spending.

Don't say *yes* so easily. Practice saying *no*. We want to share with you a dial exercise proposed by Tim Ferriss that will help you develop a more controlled and conscious relationship with money without denying its role in your life.

Think and decide what are the things you love the most and you really enjoy spending money on them (Ferriss, 2019). We are providing a short list here to help, but it could be anything else:

- travel
- clothes
- convenience
- health and fitness
- entertainment
- cars
- home & decoration stuff

Now, think about how much money you usually spend on that area of pleasure and dial it up: Increase that amount in ten. What do you think your life would be like if you could increase that much of the money you spend in your most preferred area of life? How amazing did you find that picture? Well, to get there, you need to cut down your expenses on the things you like less. The Stoic advice to handle money is "spending very little on the things you don't like, and going extravagant on the things you do" (Ferriss, 2019).

When you buy stuff, you are basically exchanging time of your life which you have taken from something else: family, friends, spare time, sleeping, taking care of your health, and so on. Therefore, you must be sure that what you exchange your money for is really worth it. As Epictetus said, don't sell yourself cheap. Don't exchange your time for worthless things.

Free Yourself From Your Thoughts

The idea of releasing yourself from your thoughts sounds a bit weird in the middle of a book that talks about philosophy which is, in fact, the art of improving your life through the power of your mind. This section isn't about stopping thinking but, instead, learning how to do it more cleverly. Setting yourself free from your thoughts implies owning them. Here there are some simple strategies to use the power of your mind instead of letting it control you and trigger undesired emotions.

Writing

When you have to think about any issue that worries you, it is difficult to center your attention specifically on the matter. Writing is a useful tool to help yourself stay focused. The simple act of putting things into words is a way to materialize your ideas and bring them from an abstract plane where you can't grab them to a concrete existence. It is a similar process to naming your challenges to finally recognize them.

Writing is better than speaking because it endows thoughts with a more tangible sense of existence. They become malleable. Once you write down your ideas, you can find connections between them, and delete the meaningless. In addition to that, writing allows you to track your processes. We have already mentioned the importance of being aware of the processes.

The technique is called journaling, and it is similar to keeping a diary. It doesn't need to be daily writing but whenever you feel the need to register what is happening. You can write about whatever you want or choose guided journals where you will find pieces of Stoics' text to read and reflect on, and then a few tasks to write about.

One influential contemporary Stoic (What is stoicism, 2018), Tim Ferris, suggests making journaling a morning habit. Taking other Stoic's words, he says, "Once we get those muddy, maddening, confusing thoughts [nebulous worries, jitters, and preoccupations] on the page, we face our day with clearer eyes" (Ferriss, 2015, para 15). He also explains that this practice doesn't intend to increase productivity but to help figure out what you are dealing with that day. It helps you make it through with a new perspective.

Meditation

There are different types of meditation and here we are going to suggest one that is consistent with the Stoic mindset. Meditation is nowadays a fashionable practice, which is good, but you have to develop a technique that serves your purposes and not just do it randomly.

Stoics suggest that meditation should help you nurture non-judgmental awareness and the ability to see what happens around you and inside you clearly and calmly. It is called mindful meditation (Ontiveros, 2019). It is a practice that has very concrete steps: You sit down, turn your look inwards, and watch attentively to your thoughts. The key here is to find the distance to avoid getting trapped by your own thoughts or being distracted by the exterior. It is all about practice. It can be difficult at first, but then it becomes simpler.

The main objective of mindful meditation is to understand that thoughts aren't the reality but a sort of lens through which you watch it. It is called cognitive fusion, and it helps you to realize that "Often the content and the emotion of thoughts become fused such that we see them not as the mental constructs they are, but as objective facts" (Ontiveros, 2019, para 5). Through mindful meditation, you can give thoughts back to the entity of your own mental production and elude considering their reality. The awareness of thoughts as a product of your mind restores the power to change them.

Walking

In Ancient Greece, walking played an important role in civilian life. People gathered in the Agora, the public place to debate, teach and learn, by walking. Diogenes of Synope, a Cynic philosopher who influenced Zeno, was, in fact, a wanderer without a home. He walked barefoot through Athens, divulging his ideas. To him, walking was a way to express and exercise freedom (Robertson, 2019).

The picture of a Stoic can be drawn as someone who is walking calmly in the middle of the crowd, being close to everybody, but letting no one obstruct their way. For ancient Stoics, the power of walking, alone or in company, was, on one hand, related to exercising the body, and on the other hand, a representation of the way to stay in the world: When you walk, you keep yourself in movement, keeping nature's pace, but not moving too fast so you can change direction whenever it is needed (Robertson, 2019).

Chapter 8:

Step 2—Stoic Approach To Becoming More Resilient

If you reached stoicism searching for a promise of constant cheerfulness, then you might be a bit disappointed. Life isn't a bed of roses. It is full of challenges and tribulations. However, it doesn't mean that stoicism has a pessimistic insight. On the contrary, challenges are the way life tells you '*You are doing good, but you can do better.*' Without difficulties and withdrawals, we would remain stuck in mediocrity and that is totally against the pursuit of virtue.

Happiness must be grounded on a realistic basis. Schopenhauer, a German philosopher of the 19th century, was a true enthusiast of pain and suffering, and he did have a pessimistic perception of life. Although stoicism doesn't agree with this perspective, we have to admit that Schopenhauer was right about the role painful situations play to make people realize and cherish happiness (Schopenhauer, 1891). In general terms, you are more aware of the moments when you are happy and when you aren't. Does it mean that you are going to love having problems or suffering? Not necessarily, but you can learn to connect differently with pain.

What Is Resilience?

All the difficult tasks you find on your way and all the losses you have to overcome, the fears and the deceptions you deal with are inevitable stop-offs in life. The key to being able to overcome them is resilience: Not just moving on despite the pain but becoming better through it.

Among the many definitions of the word, we picked the one that better reflects the Stoic principles:

> Resilience is the ability to adapt to change positively, recover from difficulties and persist in facing challenges. It's about growing stronger, not weaker after life throws you a curveball. Resilience is not a characteristic you are born with or not; it's something you build over time through intentional practices and techniques (Ogilvie, n.d., para 1)

These are just other words for what Epictetus taught about endurance and persistence, relying upon your internal fortitude, and not letting your weaknesses define you. Your vulnerabilities can be turned into your strengths.

Stoics promoted an indifferent attitude towards everything that couldn't be controlled by yourself. Nonetheless, as we discussed, it isn't rendered in indolence. Stoicism is not about denying pain but giving it the proper time instead of letting it linger. When something grievous occurs, you must give yourself the time to mourn and grieve. There isn't a formula to calculate how much it should hurt, or how long you should dedicate to suffering. Those are relative to each person and there is no right or wrong. The only guideline is the Stoic rule: Is this that I'm doing in harmony with nature? Is this my reasoned choice?

Perhaps the most helpful advice stoicism can give to enhance resilience is being aware of the painful situation you are going through. Naming and visualizing what makes you suffer is always the first step to healthily overcoming it. Resilience is what makes you recognize pain, adapt to the circumstances, and later, move forward.

When something terrible happens, it feels like the pain is going to last forever. However, you know that isn't true because you have been through similar situations before, and here you are. Marcus Aurelius wrote in his book *Meditations*: "How are negative emotions productive? Just because you are feeling this way... do you think the world cares?" (Marcus Aurelius, 2006). Practice remembering that emotions are ephemeral, and life goes on. Keep saying to yourself: This too shall pass.

The Power of Being Alone

Being lonely has a bad reputation. It is commonly associated with negative emotions such as isolation, depression, sadness, or just being antisocial. Stoicism has a totally different perspective on solitude. Being alone is, in fact, the opportunity to be with yourself, and that is great company. If you don't enjoy being with yourself, why do you think others would? If you don't learn to be with yourself, you will probably fail to be with others. Enjoying your own company is a way to improve your relationship with others.

On another hand, being alone doesn't always mean having nobody around. It can be just you in your house, and still don't feel alone, while you can be surrounded by lots of people and still feel lonely. It is the state of your mind that makes the difference.

Marcus Aurelius had another vision of loneliness. He wrote in his Meditations (2006): "There is no place as powerful for quiet and relaxation, as one's mind." When you are alone, it is easier to center your attention on yourself and hear your thoughts without distractions. You forget about others' impressions about yourself and have a real opportunity for renewal and reordering your life.

We have already talked about mindful meditation as the accurate practice for developing a Stoic mindset. There are several techniques to achieve the required level of concentration to take the greatest benefit every time you meditate, and the key is your breathing. Therefore, here you will find a breathing technique developed in Ancient Rome by Athenodorus and Marcus Aurelius:

The objective is to focus on your breathing and settle a certain rhythm to separate your mind from the external distractors. To meditate, you first need to reach a contemplative state of the mind. Ancient Romans used to repeat the alphabet while they inhale and exhale. Our alphabet doesn't make too much sense because most of the letters are composed of one syllable, so we would be breathing quite fast. Instead, you can simply count to ten. Perhaps, when you start your practice it will take you more time to concentrate, so you can count to twenty, for instance.

If you don't like numbers you can pick the days of the week, colors, or the name of the states. You have to say each word in your mind in each out-breath (Robertson, 2017). Before you notice, you will be out of this world, inside your own mind.

The Power of Sharing

As Stoics explain, human beings are intrinsically social, therefore, the need to be with peers is genuine and natural. Seneca said: "There is no enjoying the possession of anything valuable unless one has someone to share it with" (Kavli, 2017, para 2). Unlike other philosophical approaches, human beings don't live in communities just to satisfy survival needs. Even if you were self-sufficient, you would still need others. Seneca explained it through three ideas (Kavli, 2017):

- Being with others is a choice. If someone leaves your life, you will continue to live, but if you had the chance, you would rather take that person back.

- Friends and the other bonds you build aren't based on needs but a superabundance of virtue.

- Friendship and affective bonds, although they belong to the realm of the externals, don't affect your control in the search for happiness, since they are founded on virtue.

While this emphasis on sharing might seem opposed to the relevance of solitude, they are two sides of the same coin. Stoicism has the rule to explain how to combine apparently opposed ideas: Escape from the extremes and search for the golden mean. Take your time to be alone and enhance your self-acknowledgement and your self-awareness to later join your community and thrive with others.

Stoicism also highlights the importance of connecting with others. Marcus Aurelius, a man that surely had hundreds of people around and probably felt lonely, advised that every day you should have in mind two things: You are going to run into people feeling lonely, and in need of company, and among them, you will find different types of person: "the busybody, the thankless, the overbearing, the treacherous, the envious, the unneighborly" (Kavli, 2017, para 35). Even though you can decide which bonds you want to nurture and which of them are harmful to you, stoicism is a deeply human philosophy and compels you to treat others kindly.

There Is No Better Teacher Than Failure

In the previous section, we discussed how pain becomes a tool to recognize and cherish happiness. In a similar sense, the only way to relish success is by knowing failure. A Stoic statement resonates here: What stands in the way becomes the way. Therefore, any time you feel you fail, consider it the step you need to take to continue your trip toward your goals.

One of the Stoic principles was to get rid of toxic emotions, such as remorse for what could have been different. While that will lead you to nowhere, you can still focus on what you can learn from what actually happened.

Apart from that, you should review what you consider a failure: Did everything go wrong, or did it just result differently from what you expected? How do you know that what you expected was best? Stoics would tell you that if it happened, that was the best. Then, perhaps it isn't exactly a failure.

However, it is inevitable sometimes to feel disappointed when things don't go your way repeatedly. There are simple techniques to train your mind to fight against this sense of failure that is totally unnatural and unproductive. First, learn to set achievable and realistic goals. You must have a great purpose that compels you to build the best version of yourself, but that's the purpose of life. You can't wait for that to feel successful. Try to set and recognize simple daily achievements. Then, write down a gratitude list. It is very easy to identify what disturbs us, but not what makes us happy. Form a habit to put into words the things you are grateful for: health, family, job, projects, and the willingness to improve your quality of life, just to name a few.

Finally, you must pay attention to the way you treat yourself when you experience failure. Don't be so critical of yourself. Remember the Stoics' lessons: You have the possibility to make decisions, and if you searched for the reasons before acting, then your part is completed. As your instinct is to treat others kindly, you must also be nice to yourself. That is all you have.

Death: A Path That Gives Way To New Life

Most people are afraid of death, but not so many can actually tell what frightens them: Is it what you are going to find after death? Will you crave the people and things in this world? Do you feel bad about all the things you are going to miss for not being here?

Stoicism has one basic statement about death: It is inescapable. That's the only exclusive certainty all individuals can have: Life will come to an end. That sounds pretty horrible, but it is true. Stoicism is always grounded in truth. The fact of being completely aware of the finality of life is, in fact, what makes it amazing. Do you think you would enjoy the things you like if you knew they will last forever? Would you be moved to change and improve if you had an eternity to do it? This is what Marcus Aurelius (2006) thought about death: "All of us shall die, so while you live, why not be good and the best version of yourself?."

Of course, there is a difference between knowing that someday you are eventually going to die and having an idea of when that might happen. There are reasons why nature was wise enough to prevent us from the ability to predict death, and even be unconscious of it. Although most people are afraid of death, they aren't constantly thinking about it. When death bursts into someone's life, it is inevitably disturbing. It is a reminder that it can happen to anybody at any moment. You can't act like it didn't exist. There is no option to be indifferent to it because that would make you act irresponsibly.

If there is no way to escape from death but you can't waste your life hiding from it, you can, at least, learn to see it less tragically. People fear and suffer in front of death because it is assumed as the ultimate end. You think that when you die, everything is over, or when someone you love dies, you will never meet them again. Those ideas of wholeness are unbearable for human beings. Stoics invite you to think of death as a change in the matter. It is the end of one thing but the beginning of something else. We don't know what it is, but we can still be ready to accept it when it comes.

Chapter 9:

Step 3—Stoic Approach To Living

A Happier Life

Have you ever wondered what it takes you to be happy? If you found a magic lamp to rub and the genie appears but grants you unlimited wishes… How many do you think you need to be truly happy? Seneca explained that the problem doesn't lie in what you lack but in how much you wish. This means that the more you get, the more you think you need. However, the bottom line is that you already have enough to be happy (Holiday, 2019).

Reality and the frenetic rhythm of your routine can be tricky and make you think that you are running short of a lot of stuff. You are constantly bombarded with publicity selling things that promise happiness. And it is fine to want some of them, but Stoics advise not to let them become imperative issues because that is the main source of human misery.

Integrity: Aligning Intentions With Actions

We have already dedicated a few words to integrity through Epictitus's contribution to stoicism. However, integrity is a core concept in stoicism, hence, we shall delve into it and understand how it impacts your life.

Let's begin with some implicit statements in the notion of integrity (Grill, 2015)

- There is an individual and intimate commitment to behaving in correspondence to reason;
- There is a social compromise and accountability for the personal implication in collective issues;
- There is an objective motivation that directs the two latter.

In a nutshell, integrity is rendered in the perfect orientation of your actions by your intentions. In simple words, it would be to always be true to yourself, regardless of others' opinions, fashion trends, or even legal frames. Societies are ruled by a normative system, but the sense of justice is ultimately rooted in your own values. Sometimes, things that are allowed or prohibited by the law don't reflect justice. Preserving integrity implies being able to identify those situations. It doesn't mean that you will go against the law, but you will have a clear position about it coherent with your own set of values.

People's sets of values are a result of social construction and educational processes. However, the path of virtue leads you to weigh those values and see if they are consistent with your own. This is another aspect of the inward journey every Stoic takes at least, once to learn about themselves. The only way to preserve your integrity in any situation is knowing which are your core beliefs, and that is achieved through meditation and enhancing self-awareness.

Integrity is supported by two pillars: Wisdom, to have a clear understanding of the facts, and courage, to maintain yourself loyal to your beliefs. Here we shall point out that this can't be just an internal manifestation. It implicates action. Have you ever found a situation where you feel you are compelled to behave in a way you would never do if you could choose? Well, it isn't enough to be aware of that. That is the moment when you need the courage to make the right decision and act in consequence. There is always a choice.

There are some circumstances when people feel pressed to act in a certain way that contradicts their own will. Even though it commonly happens, just accepting that will bring you unrest and unhappiness. The only possible way to find peace and keep yourself on the path of virtue is to keep everything you do aligned with your purpose. And it demands walking away from some places or leaving people behind. It is simple, not easy.

In our culture, it is particularly difficult to make these decisions because we are constantly strained to avoid conflict or to knock the trend. The fear of being excluded and being alone commonly leads you to do things just to fit in. That isn't a Stoic's behavior. But don't blame yourself! You also need to nurture your sense of belonging to your community. It is just that it will be easier—and you will be happier—when you find no contradiction between what you want to do and what you actually do.

There is a skill that can also be trained to help you preserve your integrity in the smallest actions of your day. Learn to say *no.* The first lesson Zeno received from the Cynics was: People have an irrepressible tendency to say yes. And that becomes a problem because the more you admit to doing, the more difficulties you find to reject later. You must learn to say *no* and feel fine about it. Marcus Aurelius said: "If it is not RIGHT do not do it" (Kenedy, n.d. para 1). You can develop this ability to say no with this simple exercise: Every day, ask yourself *what if* you had said *no.* It is impossible that you actually want to do everything you are asked to do on a regular day at work, in the street, or with your family. When you are required to do something you disagree with, just say *no.*

To achieve success, start with small goals. Don't try to change your life by taking a turn of 180°. You will grow confident and will feel better saying *no* than agreeing to anything thoughtlessly.

Master the Art of Listening

The ethical behavior that is prescribed by the Stoic philosophy implies integrity to stay true to oneself, and an honest commitment to others. The excellence of human existence must be strived by community harmony. Individual greatness is strictly linked to humankind's greatness.

There is a helpful Stoic technique to strengthen this bond with others: Listening. Most people hear, but just a few are really listening. You probably can tell when someone is listening to you even without asking them. What about your ability to listen? When someone is talking to you, are you absolutely concentrating on the other person's speech or is your mind roaming around? As it is difficult to isolate your mind from the world to talk and listen to yourself, it is also difficult to focus on a conversation. And also, as there are techniques to develop introspective communication with yourself, you can enhance your skills as a listener and be able to fully stay with the other person.

Marcus Aurelius, the emperor of Rome, was concerned about being a good listener and wrote in his *Meditations* (2006): "Acquire the habit of attending carefully to what is being said by another, and of entering, so far as possible, into the mind of the speaker." The contemporary word for Marcus's thoughts is *empathy*: You must develop the ability to stand in the other's shoes in order to truly understand what the words they say mean to them, and not just to you. That is the difference. You listen when you can feel what the other person feels, and don't focus on what you interpret from the words (Salzgeber, 2020).

Apart from being empathetic, you have the challenge to repress your eagerness to talk. When people start a conversation, they obviously expect others to answer and comment on what they say, but it is a complex task to choose the accurate moment to make an intervention. You need to learn when it is the moment to talk, and when you are just expected to listen (Zasbeger, 2020). Besides, there are occasions when it is better to say nothing at all.

Stoics wanted to reach as many people as they could because everybody deserved to find a virtuous life, and it would represent a virtuous city. That is what made them different from the others who chose distant places and dedicated themselves to contemplation. Stoics talked at the gates of the *Agora* and walked with people to share what they had learned. Therefore, apart from listening, you can make your contribution to collective progress by teaching others something you learned.

As you read about the early Stoics' lives, you might have noticed that they all share a common pattern: They developed their ideas starting on what others had taught them. Even Zeno who created the Stoic school took lessons from other philosophers, and Seneca, for instance, assimilated many ideas from Epicurus, although he didn't agree with him. All people are likely to learn, and all have something to teach. It is an act of generosity that pushes you forward on your path to a virtuous life.

Pareto's Law: Applying The 80/20 Rule

The starting point for this is understanding that you can't have it all, and you can't do everything. You must give some things up. External stimuli seem to be constantly pushing you to do more. More than what? That isn't too clear, but you keep feeling that you aren't doing enough. The pressure of productivity is hanging over your head all the time, and it doesn't result in more or better results. You give yourself so many tasks to accomplish that you end up doing nothing or doing it wrong.

A practical technique to avoid this negative pattern of behavior is applying Pareto's rule. When Pareto described this rule, he wasn't thinking from the Stoic perspective on life. He explains that for any given fact, 80% of the result comes from 20% of the action. This relation between proportions can be applied to anything (Inch by Inch Stories, n.d.). This can be rendered in a simple statement: You will get more by doing less.

Stoics didn't promote laziness. Instead, they advocated for using time and energy on what really matters. *A lot* doesn't always—perhaps, almost never—mean *better*. Therefore, you need to establish your priorities: What must be done? What happens if this isn't accomplished? A technique that we have discussed before is very helpful: Don't think only about what will happen if you complete a task because the answer will be positive. If you do the dishes now, the kitchen will be cleaner. But, what happens if you don't do the dishes right now? Does any tragedy come up?

The next step is recognizing your limits. Let's suppose that you are a writer and are capable of writing a chapter of a book in a week. Then, set realistic deadlines instead of trying to finish a book within a month.

Let's see another practical example. What is more profitable for an entrepreneur, having 80 bad clients, or 20 loyal and wealthy ones? You guessed it: The second option, according to Pareto's law. You can implement this formula in anything in your life. If you dedicate yourself less time but are fully focused on your task, you will get better results than trying to be productive for longer periods.

Chapter 10:

Step 4—Stoic Approach To Finding Your Inner Peace

When you look around you, what do you see? Can you perceive calm? Are you able to distinguish the beauty of nature? Most of the time, you might not have that perception of what surrounds you and instead, perceive a chaotic and uncertain reality. Modern life keeps you waiting for the watch, your cell phone, the news, what is urgent for tomorrow, and what you couldn't finish yesterday. Is it possible to find peace in the middle of this mess? You can't escape your routine and just disconnect from your duties.

The answer Stoics have for you is rather simple, and it takes you back to the first chapters: Everything that happens in your environment belongs to the realm of externals, and that means that you have no control over them. Therefore, the real peace you can reasonably hope for is inner peace: Being at peace with yourself.

Peace and Compassion For Yourself

As we have discussed, stoicism isn't something you can wear on certain occasions, or keep in a drawer to use when you need it. It is a mindset that gives you a particular insight of life. But do you already know your perspective on your life? This is a broad question, and it isn't haphazard. Adopting a Stoic approach implies being aware of what you expect from your life, not in the distant future but now. Remember that stoicism prompts you to reach a state of total consciousness of the moment in time you are living. Who you are and what you want to do are settled for your *here and now*.

There is no way to find inner peace if you can't connect with the moment you are living. It is called stillness, or *ataraxia*, as the Stoics called it. To realize what your perspective on your life is, you don't need to project into the future, but ask the proper question to yourself in the present. Inner peace and stillness are of great value in a world where everything changes faster and faster, and what is a truth now, can be easily questioned tomorrow. Nowadays, contemporary Stoics have to deal with a stream of nature flowing at a higher speed.

There is a Japanese contribution to the search for happiness while you walk through this crazy world. It is called *Ikigai*, which can be rendered into "the happiness of always being busy" (Rao, 2018) or the energy that motivates you to get up and face another day every morning (Arata, 2020). The *Ikigai* can be explained as "the intersection of what you love, what you are good at, what you can be paid for, and what the world needs" (Rao, 2018, para 5) and is singular for every person. Some people have found their Ikigai and know what makes them start over as the sun comes up. Many others still haven't discovered what is their *Ikigai*, and that is a source of hopelessness and despair. If you believe you haven't found your *Ikigai*, it doesn't mean you lack a purpose. It is just that you haven't visualized it yet.

Why is it important to know your *Ikigai*? Because that will help you understand the reasons and motivations behind the things you wish. Then, you will have the opportunity to judge if that thing you lack and makes you suffer is really connected to your *Ikigai*, or if it is just a reflection of the outside world. There are four fields that you have to explore when you ask about your desires (Rao, 2018)

- Does it bring you something you love?
- Is it something required by the world, and you can provide it?
- Are you getting paid for what you do?
- Does it allow you to display your best abilities?

When you pass all your objectives through this little questionnaire you figure out which of the things are tight to your purpose in life, and which are expendable. As you ask yourself these questions, don't forget that your main purpose always points to happiness, and you can't wait for the ultimate realization of ambitious goals. Remember not to focus on the end but on the process. It is about the journey, not the destination.

Negative visualization

This is another Stoic practice that helps you deal with the unexpected odds that come up in your way. Sometimes you just let go of what you can't control, and other times you flow with the stream. However, as we have said, stoicism is a philosophy of action, not reaction, and it promotes proactivity instead of passivity. Therefore, you must be prepared for the challenges.

This technique is called negative visualization and it consists in picturing all the possible worst scenarios where you can find yourself. While at first sight, it doesn't sound consistent with the idea that whatever happens, it was the best that could happen, it is the accurate way to stay in harmony with nature.

Here's an example: If you live in a hurricane zone, you must take some precautions that people who live anywhere else don't need to. When a hurricane comes, it will cause damage, but if you are prepared, that damage is going to be less severe. You can't blame nature, but you are accountable for having provisions and shelter. During Marcus Aurelius's reign, there was a flood and a plague that he couldn't stop but he still had to make decisions to deal with them.

You can implement negative visualization in any aspect of your life: If you are going on a trip, if you are launching a new project, if you are breaking up with your partner, anything. You must try to imagine all the things that could go wrong, and eventually will go wrong if you don't do this exercise and just go on improvising. For instance, if you are going on a trip, you could get ill at your destination. Knock on wood you won't but, if you do, you need to have travel medical insurance.

Although it sounds a bit pessimistic, it is exactly the opposite. Negative visualization isn't the same as always expecting the worst because it is a deliberate action to be aware of what challenges you will face and be prepared to overcome them successfully. It is a tool to empower you and strengthen your self-confidence.

Self-Discipline

Adopting stoicism as your way of life will lead you to discover a new sense of wellness. However, it isn't easy to keep yourself constant while you apply Stoic principles to rule your life. It takes great effort to enhance your self-discipline. Marcus Aurelius said: "Be like the Rocky headland on which waves constantly break. It stands firm and round it the seething waters are laid to rest" (Harshwardhan, 2019, para 18). However, the process to achieve the firmness of the rock to withstand the clashes of reality demands a lot of willpower and self-control.

Self-discipline doesn't grow instantaneously, and discipline usually behaves like a muscle: It gets tired. Those are the moments when you must be attentive the most to recover the path you have already traced for yourself. When you begin to train in meditation, it is quite common that before reaching full concentration, your mind keeps getting distracted by any thought or external issue. Then, what you do to continue to meditate, is to grab something that pushes you to a particular center: A voice, when it is a guided meditation, the rhythm of your breathing, or a mantra, in the case of yoga meditation. To train your self-discipline, it works similarly: You outline the habits to develop and keep on practicing.

Marcus Aurelius said that to gain self-discipline you must keep yourself sober and relaxed. This implies, on one hand, avoiding all the things you can get but don't really need. And, on another hand, escaping from people or situations that disturb you. Those are all externals that will just direct your energy in the wrong direction.

Even though it isn't easy to change your life and incorporate a whole set of new Stoic habits, try to simplify it by thinking about it as a dichotomy. You have formed new habits and have just two choices: You make them or break them. To go a bit further, instead of thinking about the good that you will gain if you make them a habit, remember all the pain you had before you introduced stoicism into your life. What will happen if you don't do them?

Self-reflection

When talking about self-reflection, we refer to the constant exercise of looking inwards at yourself to see if what you think, say, and do reflect the Stoic perspective of life. This attitude of self-control is not assumed with the intention of censoring or punishing yourself. It is a part of the process of self-awareness.

The first steps to self-reflection are the most difficult because you don't know where to start. Here you find some guidelines to help you:

- Set small, achievable goals. As Marcus Aurelius said (2006) "Less is more."
- Break your molds and get rid of your preconceptions.
- Put yourself in touch with nature and learn from it to know yourself.
- Dedicate more time to those little things that make you happy, like listening to music or playing with your pet. Seize the moment.
- Let the past go, and don't overthink about the future.
- Be kind to yourself. Being patient with the world and with others becomes senseless if you can't be patient and compassionate with yourself.

Apart from these pieces of advice, here you will find two practical techniques to help you:

A 'Ta-Da' list: Instead of the typical 'To-do' list that reminds you of everything you should have done but haven't yet, you will use a 'Ta-da' list to name all the things that you actually did. If the first type makes you feel ashamed or guilty, the second will trigger pride and satisfaction.

A 'What's-not-working' list: Even though there is nothing wrong with failing and not being able to accomplish some of your tasks, it is important to work on solutions to fix them. This list will help you visualize the reasons why things aren't working. Instead of feeling stressed or discouraged, you will drive your energy into finding realistic solutions.

Conclusion

When you started reading this book, you were looking for some clues to living a happier life. You might have been curious about how this philosophy developed over two thousand years ago could be helpful for you, a citizen of the 21st century. Throughout the chapters, you have realized that stoicism is about the deepest essence of human nature. The core of stoicism can be summarized in a few simple statements:

- You have the power to control your life.
- Emotions and thoughts are a creation of your mind and not reality, therefore, they can be changed.
- You can find happiness by achieving virtue based on the four pillars: Prudence, temperance, courage, and justice.
- Human beings are naturally free and endowed with reason. Therefore, everything you do is a result of a decision.
- You must learn to live in harmony with nature.
- It is all about action, and not reaction.

While these principles appear to be abstract, you have read the story of the former Stoics that originated the philosophical school, and through their examples, you learned that stoicism isn't a sophisticated system of ideas but a way to be in this world. Stoicism provides you with answers to everyday matters that can be easily adapted to any circumstance. Apart from that, stoicism also contributes to the accurate questions you should ask yourself to identify what your real purpose in life is.

Stoicism is an invitation to embrace life and enjoy every single moment, intensely and consciously. It helps you focus on what is relevant and let go of those things that just bring you pain and distress.

Every human being is a manifestation of the greatness of the universe and humankind, and every person deserves to find peace and happiness. Now, you know that both things aren't waiting for you at any unreachable place: The path to peace and happiness is right inside you.

This book has also tried to equip you with a set of practical tools to introduce the Stoic principles effectively into your life. Living philosophically doesn't mean spending your time contemplating and reflecting on absolute truths. Instead, it is about being aware that your life has a purpose. Adopting the Stoic mindset provides you with practical resources to cope with the constant challenges you inevitably find your way. Instead of giving up, they become a source of motivation for you to thrive.

The guidelines to live like a Stoic can't be learned by heart: They need to be put into practice, every day, little by little. And remember Epictetus's words: Persist and resist. One of the most helpful techniques to grasp the Stoic mindset and implement it in your life is journaling. The art of writing is rendering thoughts into tangible words. It turns ideas into matter. Journaling has two principal benefits: It helps to develop the habit, and it allows you to track your journey. Your journal is just meant to be read by you, and that is valuable information to be more self-aware of how well you are doing it.

Thank You

As we come to the end of our journey together, I want to express my gratitude for your decision to read 'Stoicism Made Simple'. I understand that there are countless books on the subject of Stoicism to choose from, and I'm honored that you selected this one.

Your commitment to reading until the very end is truly appreciated, and I hope that you found the content engaging and thought-provoking. If you enjoyed the book, I would be immensely grateful if you could take a few moments to leave a review on Amazon (or Goodreads). You can scan the QR code below to be taken to a review page on Amazon.

Your feedback would be incredibly valuable and help other readers discover this book. Once again, thank you for choosing 'Stoicism Made Simple' and for allowing me to be a part of your journey.

Kindest Regards,

Terry Cole

References

Aperture (2021) Stoicism: Become Undefeatable (Video) https://www.youtube.com/watch?v=EFkyxzJtiv4

Arata, S. (2020) Ikigai: Find Your Purpose in 5 Steps. (Video) Arata Academy English. https://www.youtube.com/watch?v=iPYvZoYSb9o

Bele, T. (2021) *Mastering the Stoic Virtues.* Search Medium. https://medium.com/stoicism-philosophy-as-a-way-of-life/mastering-the-stoic-virtues-1ffbb6fb5a96#:~:text=Prudence%2C%20Temperance%2C%20Courage%2C%20and,with%20the%20body%20of%20nature.

Benjamin Personal Power (2020) The Stoic Approach to Working Out. (Video) https://www.youtube.com/watch?v=Mh3W5cICbQQ

Bertoloti, J.W. (2022) *How to Be Invincible—According to the Stoics.* Search Medium. https://medium.com/perennial/responding-to-criticism-and-insults-according-to-the-stoics-71d25d6c6801

Biographics (2020) Marcus Aurelius The Philosopher King. (Video) https://www.youtube.com/watch?v=IdLPzv66OYQ

Bologna, F. (2021) *Who was Nero?* British Museum. https://www.britishmuseum.org/blog/who-was-nero

Cleary, C. (n.d.) How to Be a Stoic: Using Ancient Philosophy to Live a Modern Life: a review. *The Philosophers' Magazine Archive.* https://archive.philosophersmag.com/how-to-be-a-stoic-using-ancient-philosophy-to-live-a-modern-life-a-review/

Cohn, P. (2023) *Performing at a Higher Level | Sports Psychology Articles.* Peak Performance Sports. https://www.peaksports.com/sports-psychology-blog/the-mindset-to-perform-at-a-higher-level/

Daily Stoic (n.d.) *The Transformation of Stoicism Over The Centuries: An Interview With Historian Ada Palmer.* https://dailystoic.com/the-transformation-of-stoicism-over-the-centuries-an-interview-with-historian-ada-palmer/

Daily Stoic (n.d.b) *Your Weakness Can Be Your Strength.* https://dailystoic.com/your-weakness-can-be-your-strength/

Daily Stoic (n.d.c) *Alive Time Challenge Day 1: Physical Exercise.* https://dailystoic.com/alive-time-challenge-day-1-physical-exercise/#:~:text=Fitness%20was%20essential.,has%20less%20patience%20for%20others.

Daily Stoic (2020) Who is Seneca? (Rome's Greatest Stoic Thinker) [Video] https://www.youtube.com/watch?v=J3wZoqElCgs

Desauteles, R. (2018) *No man ever steps in the same river twice. For it's not the same river and he's not the same man.* Bob Desauteles. https://www.bobdesautels.com/blog/2018/8/6/no-man-ever-steps-in-the-same-river-twice-for-its-not-the-same-river-and-hes-not-the-same-man-heraclitus

Diaz, A. (2020) *Aristotle's Golden Mean and the Role of Moderation.* Bahai Teachings. https://bahaiteachings.org/aristotles-golden-mean-role-of-moderation/

Dobbin, R. & Graver, M. (2021) *Epictetus.* Stanford Encyclopedia of Philosophy. https://plato.stanford.edu/entries/epictetus/

Einzelgänger (2020) Stoicism. Zeno's lost philosophy. [Video] https://www.youtube.com/watch?v=szUsitFuF9c

Ferriss, T. (2015) *What My Morning Journal Looks Like*. The Tim Ferriss Show. https://tim.blog/2015/01/15/morning-pages/

Ferriss, T. (2018) Fear-Setting: The Most Important Exercise I Still Do Today [Video] https://www.youtube.com/watch?v=o7EVMjgsSME

Garrett, J. (2021) *What is Stoicism? Explained in 3 Beliefs. The Collector.* https://www.thecollector.com/what-is-stoicism-the-stoics-beliefs/

Grill, C. (2015) *The stoics on integrity*. The Integrity Project. https://integrityproject.org/2015/01/14/the-stoics-on-integrity/

Hanselman, S. (n.d.) *The 9 Core Stoic Beliefs.* Daily Stoic. https://dailystoic.com/9-core-stoic-beliefs/

Harshwardhan, S. (2019) Article is about using Meditations (by Marcus Aurelius) to help oneself deal with challenges in life. https://www.elephantjournal.com/2019/03/article-is-about-using-meditations-by-marcus-aurelius-to-help-oneself-deal-with-challenges-in-life/

Hobsbawm, E. (1995) *A history of the 20th century.* https://files.libcom.org/files/Eric%20Hobsbawm%20-%20Age%20Of%20Extremes%20-%201914-1991.pdf

Holiday, R. & Hanselman, S. (n.d.) *Glossary.* Daily Stoic. https://dailystoic.com/glossary/#:~:text=Eupatheia%20(%CE%B5%E1%BD%90%CF%80%CE%AC%CE%B8%CE%B5%CE%B9%CE%B1)%3A%20good%20passions,joy%20is%20rational%20elation%20.%20.%20.

Holiday, R. (2019) Seneca: 5 Practices Of Stoicism For A Better Life. [Video] Daily Stoic. https://www.youtube.com/watch?v=O1bfB972bT0

Inch by Inch Stories (n.d.) *Pareto Principle 80/20 Rule.* https://inchbyinchstories.com/pareto-principle-80-20-rule/

Internet Encyclopedia of Philosophy (n.d.) *Ancient Greek Philosophy.* https://iep.utm.edu/ancient-greek-philosophy/#H5

Jones, P. (2015) *How ancient Athens handled immigrants.* The Spectator. https://www.spectator.co.uk/article/how-ancient-athens-handled-immigrants/

Kamtekar, R. (2017) *Marcus Aurelius.* Stanford Encyclopedia of Philosophy. https://plato.stanford.edu/entries/marcus-aurelius/

Kavli, H. (2017) *Some Stoic Musings on Loneliness by Kevin Vost.* Modern stoicism. https://modernstoicism.com/some-stoic-musings-on-loneliness-by-kevin-vost/

Kennedy, V. (n.d.) *Integrity Has No Need Of Rules.* Daily Stoic. https://dailystoic.com/integrity/

Kings and Generals (2020) Marco Aurelio - Emperador Filósofo: Fin de la Edad de Oro Romana (Video) https://www.youtube.com/watch?v=cLtDWIsOs1E

Let's talk philosophy (2019) Zeno of Citium | Founder Of Stoicism (Video) https://www.youtube.com/watch?v=Gu0FrhJ3HE4

Loeb, J. & Henderson, J. (n.d.) *Seneca the younger.* Epistles. https://www.loebclassics.com/view/seneca_younger-epistles/1917/pb_LCL075.39.xml?readMode=recto

Marcus Aurelius (2006) *Meditations.* Penguin UK. https://books.google.com.ar/books?id=udApd8ZGIV0C&dq=%E2%80%9CJust+as+you+yourself+are+a+complementary+part+of+a+social+system,+so+too+your+every+action+should+complement+a+life+of+social+principle.+If+any+action+of+yours,+then,+does+not+have+dire

ct+or+indirect+relation+to+the+social+end,+it+pulls+your+life+apart+and+destroys+its+unity.%E2%80%9D&hl=es&source=gbs_navlinks_s

Mark, J. (2011) *Zeno of Citium.* World History Encyclopedia. https://www.worldhistory.org/Zeno_of_Citium/

Mark, J. (2021) *Agora.* World history Encyclopedia. https://www.worldhistory.org/agora/

MedlinePlus (2022) *Stress and your health.* https://medlineplus.gov/ency/article/003211.htm

Merriam-Webster Dictionary (n.d.) *Challenge.* https://www.merriam-webster.com/dictionary/challenge

Mr. Smart (2020a) Epictetus - His life, Stoic Philosophy, Quotes & his book Discourses | Stoic Philosophy. [Video] https://www.youtube.com/watch?v=mwLm2bROkLQ

Mr. Smart (2020b) 15 Lessons from the Enchiridion (Handbook) of Epictetus | Quotes & Book Summary [Video] https://www.youtube.com/watch?v=cgdYW-YyoNM

Mr. Smart (2020c) 9 Stoic lessons of Marcus Aurelius from Meditations. [Video] https://www.youtube.com/watch?v=EtEL486FEkw&t=0s

Nerdish App (n.d.) *Brief Ancient Greece history and facts.* https://nerdish.io/topics/ancient-greece-a-brief-guide-to-the-history-culture-and-daily-life/

Ogilvie, E. (n.d.) *What Is Resilience? How Is It Defined?* Resilience Development Company. https://www.resiliencetraining.co.uk/what-is-resilience/

Ontiveros, C. (12019) *Why Stoics Should Meditate.* Stoa Conversations. https://stoameditation.com/blog/why-stoics-should-meditate/

Pigliucci, M. (2018) Stoicism as a philosophy for an ordinary life. (Video) TEDx Talks. https://www.youtube.com/watch?v=Yhn1Fe8cT0Q

Pursuit of Wonder (2022) The Art of Caring Less - The Philosophy of Baruch Spinoza. (Video) https://www.youtube.com/watch?v=rwO3splR8rk

Rao, M. (2018) *Ikigai, flow and longevity: what the Japanese can teach the world.* Your Story. https://yourstory.com/2018/12/ikigai-flow-longevity-japanese-teachings

Robertson, D. (2017) An ancient stoic meditation technique. https://donaldrobertson.name/2017/03/22/an-ancient-stoic-meditation-technique/#:~:text=Say%20one%20word%20or%20number,passage%20from%20Marcus%20Aurelius%20above.

Robertson, D. (2019) *How to Walk Like a Stoic.* Search Medium. https://medium.com/stoicism-philosophy-as-a-way-of-life/how-to-walk-like-a-stoic-e1a41c8d5af0

Salzgeber, J. (2020) *The art of listening.* The Stoic Gym. https://thestoicgym.com/the-stoic-magazine/article/51

Sharpe, M. & Blackford, R. (2017) *Stoicism 5.0: The unlikely 21st century reboot of an ancient philosophy.* The Conversation. https://theconversation.com/stoicism-5-0-the-unlikely-21st-century-reboot-of-an-ancient-philosophy-80986

Schopenhauer, A. (1891) *On the Sufferings of the World.* https://www.atlasofplaces.com/essays/on-the-sufferings-of-the-world/

Smiley, C. (1934) Stoicism and Its Influence on Roman Life and Thought. *The Classical Journal,* 29(9), pp. 645-657. https://www.jstor.org/stable/3289820?read-now=1#page_scan_tab_contents

Stanford Encyclopedia of Philosophy (2020) *Baruch Spinoza.* https://plato.stanford.edu/entries/spinoza/

Stanford Encyclopedia of Philosophy (2023) *Stoicism.* https://plato.stanford.edu/entries/stoicism/#RenaEarlModePhil

Vargas, D. (2022) *How a Stoic Views Self-Care of Their Mind and Body.* Stoic Sage. https://www.stoicsage.co/post/how-a-stoic-views-self-care-of-their-mind-and-body

What is Stoicism? (n.d.) *How to Keep a Stoic Journal - 7 Days of Example Entries.* https://whatisstoicism.com/stoicism-resources/how-to-keep-a-stoic-journal-7-days-of-example-entries/

World Health Organization (2023) *Stress.* https://www.who.int/news-room/questions-and-answers/item/stress

Wycherley, R.E. (1978) *The Stones of Athens.* Princeton Legacy Library. https://books.google.com.ar/books?id=9qh9BgAAQBAJ&printsec=frontcover&hl=es#v=onepage&q&f=false

Made in the USA
Las Vegas, NV
25 August 2023

76578045R00069